Exploring Nonfiction with Young Learners

Darla Miner and Jill Zitnay

ROWMAN & LITTLEFIELD EDUCATION
A division of
ROWMAN & LITTLEFIELD PUBLISHERS, INC.
Lanham • New York • Toronto • Plymouth, UK

Published by Rowman & Littlefield Education
A division of Rowman & Littlefield Publishers, Inc.
A wholly owned subsidary of The Rowman & Littlefield Publishing Group, Inc.
4501 Forbes Boulevard, Suite 200, Lanham, Maryland 20706
www.rowman.com

10 Thornbury Road, Plymouth PL6 7PP, United Kingdom

British Library Cataloguing in Publication Information Available

Library of Congress Cataloging-in-Publication Data

Miner, Darla, 1967–
  Exploring nonfiction with young learners / Darla Miner and Jill Zitnay.
    p. cm.
  Includes bibliographical references.
  ISBN 978-1-61048-493-0 (cloth : alk. paper)—ISBN 978-1-61048-494-7 (pbk. : alk. paper)—ISBN 978-1-61048-495-4 (electronic)
 1. Language arts (Elementary). 2. English language—Composition and exercises—Study and teaching (Primary). 3. English language—Composition and exercises—Study and teaching (Elementary). 4. Exposition (Rhetoric). 5. Creative nonfiction. I. Zitnay, Jill, 1968– II. Title.
  LB1139.5.L35 M56 2012
  372.47—dc23   2012002364

∞™ The paper used in this publication meets the minimum requirements of American National Standard for Information Sciences—Permanence of Paper for Printed Library Materials, ANSI/NISO Z39.48-1992.

Printed in the United States of America

Dedication from Darla Taylor Miner

I'd like to dedicate this book to all of my colleagues and administrators who inspired me to strive for all of my goals. A special thanks goes out to my current principal, Michael Gray, and former principal, Kathleen Sheehy, for giving me the time and opportunity to pursue my passions. I'd also like to dedicate this book to my loving husband, Eric, and my two daughters, Ashley and Mackenzie. Their patience and support enabled me to write this book with success. Finally, to my parents, Kenneth and Gina Taylor, sister, Lesley Nappi, and good friends Nancy Woolfrey, Coral Hardman, and Shari Chase, for checking in on me to make sure I got this done!

Dedication from Jill Zitnay

I would like to dedicate this book to my loving God, who sustains me; to my husband, Jeff, who encourages me to persevere; and to my extraordinary children, Joshua and Jordan. Also to my parents, Bill and Nancy Noga, and my sister, Tracy, who always support me. Finally, to my friend Esmee, who taught me to have this dream and reach for it. Thank you to everyone who has touched my life.

CONTENTS

INTRODUCTION

WHY TEACH NONFICTION?

Did you know that almost all of what we read and write in the real world is nonfiction. Yet, almost all read-alouds for primary students are fiction picture books and about 90 percent of guided reading libraries are composed of fiction. So why teach the youngest readers how nonfiction is organized?

Here's one important reason: By the time they reach fourth grade, most students will be reading nonfiction at three reading recovery levels below that of their fiction reading. That means that many students will have difficulty understanding what they read in subjects such as science and social studies. Early practice in nonfiction text structure skills—those clues that navigate readers through expository text—is simply essential for later success in school.

Even though we spend most of our time reading nonfiction, the transition from reading fiction to nonfiction should begin in early elementary school. Reading nonfiction requires the ability to access accurate background knowledge, connect facts, identify structure, and navigate access features. When reading nonfiction, children will connect to their background knowledge to make sense of new content. If this background knowledge is absent or inaccurate, new learning will be difficult, so it is critical that teachers provide correct background knowledge.

Children also have difficulty making connections while reading nonfiction because facts are often presented without cohesion. That is, students are not able to recognize relationships in nonfiction texts, such as cause and effect, on their own. Children may also have difficulty comprehending nonfiction because, unlike fiction, which has one basic structure, nonfiction has eight structures: descriptive, recount, procedural, explanatory, comparison, response, causation, and persuasive.

Nonfiction is also full of features (such as charts, photographs, and captions) and text cues that signal important concepts and scaffold understanding for the reader. These features, rarely found in fiction, provide explicit clues to help readers sift essential information from less important details. By teaching how to use these features, students learn how to navigate text and use access features to manage and comprehend information that is presented in nonfiction.

This book provides a teacher-friendly resource to identify nonfiction text structures as well as understand text access features to teach students how to comprehend nonfiction.

WHAT THIS BOOK COVERS

This resource explores the four basic nonfiction structures that the youngest learners are most likely to encounter as they read and begin to write: descriptive, recount/collection, procedural, and explanatory. The book also includes information to help teach four more complex structures that younger readers sometimes encounter during read-alouds: comparison, response, causation (or cause and effect), and persuasive genres.

How Exploring Nonfiction with Young Learners Is Organized

This book is organized to help teachers plan lessons using each type of nonfiction structure. Strategies and suggestions for activities to use before, during, and after reading are included. Templates and graphic organizers are also provided to facilitate planning and offer additional resources.

What's in This Book

This book contains detailed information about each text structure as well as mentor texts to illustrate each type. Text structures and text access features are defined and located in easy reference charts. Whole class and small group planning ideas are included throughout the book to allow for differentiation. Additionally, assessment ideas, sample think-alouds, lesson-planning templates, and sample lessons with completed graphic organizers are included for each text structure.

How to Use This Book

The lessons in this book are organized in a before/during/after reading format so that a skill can be introduced to the students, practiced with them, and then reinforced independently. Once skills have been introduced and practiced, they can be reinforced throughout the day in other subject areas. Science, social studies, and math provide perfect opportunities to reinforce and review nonfiction text structures. You may also use the materials from these subject areas to introduce and teach the structures during your literacy block. These multiple exposures help students begin to automatically apply the text clues to comprehend meaning.

This book also clearly defines different nonfiction text structures and text access features to help you prepare lessons for students. Text structures define a genre. Defining the differences help students read better for information. Is the structure of the text procedural (step-by-step instructions on how to perform a task), or is it a recount (retelling of a person's life or an event)? Each structure also contains specific text features, such as headings, charts, or captions. What text features are present to facilitate understanding? Are there headings, pictures with captions, or charts that I can draw students' attention to?

Suggestions for planning multiple lessons with the same texts are given throughout this book. When you plan a lesson for a nonfiction piece of text, it is important to focus on the text structure as well as one or two text access features. You can even use the same text to teach multiple lessons. For example, you may introduce new vocabulary and access features, such as table of contents and glossary, on day 1, then tackle other access features, such as graphs and diagrams, on day 2. As students become familiar with the text, they will be able to focus on the new skills being introduced to them more easily. Varying your lessons with the same text will maintain the students' interest as they explore the structure and access features presented.

Learning how to organize lessons into a before/during/after format will help to explicitly teach the topic, text structure, and access features. Clear strategies and examples are provided for before, during, and after portions of the lessons to guide you as you prepare to explore nonfiction with your students.

ONE

WHAT MAKES
NONFICTION UNIQUE?

Nonfiction differs from fiction in that each nonfiction text can take the form of many structures. Most fiction is organized with a beginning/middle/end format and includes characters, problems, and solutions. However, nonfiction can take the form of several structures, such as a main idea with supporting details, a timeline, a sequence of step-by-step directions, or a question-and-answer format. Moreover, nonfiction text tends to teach something and give information that is true, versus fictional text, which is fully inspired by imagination.

WHAT ARE NONFICTION TEXT STRUCTURES?

The term *text structure* refers to the organizational patterns of nonfiction text that serve as a framework. Nonfiction text structures have different patterns, each of which helps the reader comprehend the important information in the text. Students have an easier time comprehending fiction text because they are familiar with the structure, or the beginning/middle/end format. Understanding the structure of a text facilitates comprehension.

Children know what to expect when they read fiction. They innately piece a story together based on their understanding of text structure. As discussed earlier, children have difficulty understanding nonfiction material because texts can appear in a variety of structures. Children become confused by different organizational patterns, and they have difficulty connecting information as they read. To facilitate comprehension, students must understand each type of nonfiction structure. The four basic nonfiction text structures that young readers are most likely to encounter are descriptive, recount, procedural, and explanatory. These structures are defined as follows.

A descriptive text tells about a topic. This type of text is structured with a main idea with supporting details. You may choose to read a description when you are teaching a specific topic to the class. For example, you may choose several books about insects when you are studying insects. Students will learn many facts while reading a description on a specific topic.

A recount text tells about a specific person or event. It is organized as a series through time. You may choose a recount if you are teaching students about a famous person. Recounts contain a series of events that pertain to the person or event that the text focuses on. You may choose to read a recount (biography) about a famous author to your students after you complete an author study. Other recounts may present a topic through a series of time.

A procedural text explains how to do something, or it gives directions on how to perform a task. Young students experience procedural text inside and outside books. When you provide simple step-by-step charts for an art lesson or class activity, you are exposing your students to procedural text. You are also exposing students to procedural text in cooking recipes or in process explanations in science, such as how to make a seed grow. The recount and procedural text structures may also be referred to as a *sequence structure*.

An explanatory text tells why things happen. Young readers love to ask why. They want to know why the sky is blue or why some animals have stripes. Explanatory books really pique their curiosity. You may choose an explanatory text to add depth to a topic you are teaching in the classroom.

See the bibliography for examples of books for each text structure.

More complex text structures are explained in chapter 7.

WHAT ARE TEXT ACCESS FEATURES?

As you can see, nonfiction differs from fiction in that it can be formatted into different text structures (table 1.1). While fiction may contain features known as story elements (setting, characters, problem), nonfiction contains several types of text access features. These features are provided to

Table 1.1

Structure	Characteristics	Example
Descriptive	Tells about a topic	Books that describes a topic such as weather, animals, or plants
Recount	Tells about a specific person or event	A biography or a book that contains a timeline of an event
Procedural	Directions on how to perform a task	A book with step-by-step instructions or a recipe book
Explanatory	Tells why things happen	A book of questions and answers

Table 1.2

Text Access Feature	What Is It? Describe It!	How Does It Help? How Do You Use It?
Glossary	An alphabetical collection of specialist terms and their meanings, usually in the form of an appendix to a book.	A preview of the glossary can aid in understanding of the text and can build schema. It is also used during reading as the terms come up to help the reader comprehend and build vocabulary.
Index	An alphabetical list—usually at the end of a book—of people, places, or topics, giving the page numbers on which they are mentioned.	Allows the reader to get to specific information in an expedient way. Useful in multitopic texts when only partial use of the text is desired. An index can also be used during prereading or reference rereading on a topic for understanding.
Table of contents	An arrangement of information or data into columns and rows or a condensed list.	Helps build schema when read before the text. Readers can formulate questions that will be answered in the text. They can also make predictions about what will be learned. The table of contents is also used when rereading about specific information is desired.
Headings	Something that forms the head, top, edge, or front of something, especially as a title for a paragraph, section, chapter, or page.	Useful to point out if the topic is large. History text often has a heading of a period or ruler, and then the following information is topic specific. This is a good time to recount or build schema.
Subheading	A heading or title subordinate to the main one.	Helps summarize information and enables readers to locate information after they read the text—students can skim the text until they find the section they are looking for.
Activity	Something that somebody takes part in or does.	Gives hands-on learning experience with the subject of the text. Another way for comprehension to occur.
Connection	The joining together of two or more people, things, or parts.	Two areas, usually the past and present, put together on a page. A model of connecting that students can do individually.
Fact	A piece of information such as a statistic or a statement of the truth.	Useful to use as a beginning reference point or a way to trigger learned information. It is easier for some students to learn from a list of facts than from a narrative.
Diagram	A simple drawing showing the basic shape, layout, or workings of something.	Helps by giving a detailed visual so students do not have to rely on the text and their own picturing to know what something looks like.
Caption	A short description or title accompanying an illustration in a printed text.	Useful when skimming or summarizing the text.

Photograph	An image produced on light-sensitive film or array inside a camera, especially a print or slide made from the developed film or from a digitized array image, or a reproduction in a newspaper, magazine, or book.	Great for previewing and summarizing. Gives readers another way to get additional details.
Illustration	A drawing, photograph, or diagram that accompanies and complements a printed, spoken, or electronic text.	Great for previewing and summarizing; gives readers another way to get additional details. Useful when photographs are not available, as with dinosaurs.
Label	A word or phrase used to describe a person, group, or parts of a thing.	Helpful in eliminating confusion when there are many points of interest in a visual.
Bullet	A large printed dot used to highlight items in a printed list.	Makes for clear concise reading.

clarify information for the reader. Examples of text access features include headings, charts, or photographs with captions. Different access features are found throughout each type of nonfiction text structure.

Nonfiction text access features provide clues that help the youngest readers and writers to figure out the meaning of the text. These features can be context clues, key (or content) vocabulary, as well as structural and graphic features. When you explicitly teach students how to recognize these critical nonfiction attributes, you give them an important strategy that will help them understand nonfiction.

Table 1.2 is a complete list of text access features that will be encountered within various structures of nonfiction text. Our youngest learners may not be exposed to all of these structures, but we included them all for you to reference. Some access features that are most common in early grades include a table of contents, index, glossary, headings, photographs, illustrations, labels, captions, activities, simple diagrams, measurements, font, and sidebars.

Remember, as used in this book, the term *text structure* refers to the organizational pattern of nonfiction text that serves as a framework. Each type of nonfiction text structure has a different pattern that helps the reader comprehend the important information in the text. The term *text access feature* refers to the features within the text that provide or clarify information, such as charts, photographs, or captions.

Choosing good literature plays a key role in teaching nonfiction. Books must have a clear text structure and contain access features to focus on. In chapter 3, we talk about how to choose books for instruction and how to code your classroom library so that students can easily access various types of books.

Two

Why Is Nonfiction
So Difficult to Comprehend?

UNDERSTANDING COHESIVE TIES

What is coherence? "The ability to understand individual sentences, and to link the ideas in a given sentence to ideas in the sentences that come before and after it" (Carlisle and Rice 2002).

We often find that students have difficulty comprehending nonfiction books, articles, and even cloze passages. Yet, when we read the same passages, we often wonder what it is about them that makes understanding so difficult for young students. An element that you will find in abundance in fiction texts is not present in most nonfiction texts. That element is the use of cohesive ties, or conjunctions. These connecting words not only tie information together but signal cause and effect or changes in meaning.

Some common cohesive ties (table 2.1) include *because, so, as a result,* and so on. Without the presence of cohesive ties in text, students lose comprehension unless they are able to infer these ties on their own. Teachers must provide scaffolding to show students how to determine the point of inference in nonfiction text.

Table 2.1   Common Cohesive Ties

Temporal	Conjunctions
First	But
Next	So
Then	However
After that	As a result
Finally	While
Before	Actually
	Instead
	Also

USING STRUCTURE-SPECIFIC SIGNAL WORDS

Different structures of nonfiction often use different signal words that allow students to infer meaning. However, if students do not know how to use these words, they will lose comprehension. Common signal words used in each text structure are included in table 2.2.

ACTIVITIES TO TEACH COHESIVE TIES AND SIGNAL WORDS

To enable students to become familiar with cohesive ties and their importance to comprehension, guidance and practice must be provided.

In the classroom, create a chart of cohesive ties and signal words to be referred to during group lessons as well as independent practice. Group these words according to text structure as indicated in table 2.2. Students may also include lists of cohesive ties and signal words in their writing notebooks.

The following is a list of activities to help build student understanding of cohesive ties and signal words. These activities may be done as a whole

Table 2.2 Common Signal Words

Descriptive/ Explanatory	Recount/Procedural Sequence	Response Problem/Solution	Comparison Persuasive	Causation Cause/Effect
For example	First	The problem is	However	If/then
Characteristics	Next	A solution is	Different	Cause/reason
For instance	Then	If/then	Still	Reasons why
Such as	Second	Because	Rather than	As a result
Is like	Third	So that	Instead of	Results or effects
Including	Before	Question/answer	Nevertheless	Therefore
To illustrate	Finally	Puzzle is solved	On the other hand	Because
For instance	After	Therefore	But	Consequently
Also	Now	As a result	Similarly	Since
And	Eventually	Consequently	Although	So
Specifically	Previously	Solve	Also	For this reason
It means	Actual use of dates		In contrast	In order to
			Alike	Affects
			Both	Hence
			All	Due to
			Same as	Thus
			Or	Leads to
			In the same way	
			Just like	
			In comparison	
			Yet	
			Unlike	

group minilesson, a small group activity, or a reinforcing center activity when students become proficient.

Activity: What Goes Here?

- Choose sentences from a familiar text.
- Present the sentences without the cohesive ties (sentence strips, interactive white board, etc.).
- Write cohesive ties on word cards.
- Have students read the sentences and choose words to fill in the blanks.
- Have students justify their answers.

Activity: But . . . So . . .

- You may want to begin with only two words (*but, so*).
- Choose three students to stand in a line in front of the class.
- Provide the first student with a sentence to say. (You may make up sentences or use sentences from a story.)
- The second student is given cohesive tie signs one at a time.
- The third student is asked to complete the sentence—for example,
  o I wanted to go to my friend's house, *but* the car wouldn't start.
  o The car wouldn't start, *so* I walked to my friend's house.
  o I wanted to make a peanut butter sandwich, *but* all the bread was gone.
  o The bread was gone, *so* I made soup for lunch instead.
- First, the three students say the sentence.
- Next, the students hold hands as they say the sentence.
- Finally, the rest of the class recites the sentence with the students.
- You can extend this activity by adding other cohesive ties (e.g., *but, so, and, because, after, if, then, before*).

Activity: Put Them Together

- Write sentences onto sentence strips or interactive white board.
- Display word cards containing cohesive ties.
- Have two students stand in front of the group.
- Give each student a sentence strip (choose two that will make sense when combined).
- Choose a third student to select the cohesive tie that puts the two sentences together.
- Read the new sentence as a group.
- Do this multiple times and have the students type or write out the completed sentences.

Cohesive ties and signal words may be reinforced through center activities. Students may sort words according to meaning, use, or corresponding text structure. The use of bingo, memory, and word puzzle/word search games can increase student awareness of these important words.

Remember that another important aspect of planning when teaching nonfiction to young learners is to embed the awareness and use of cohesive ties and signal words that may appear in the text.

Three
Getting Ready to Teach Nonfiction

WHEN TO TEACH NONFICTION

Explicit instruction with nonfiction text structures can become part of your reader's workshop or literacy block or during science, social studies, or even math instruction. Choosing texts that align with your curriculum provides the key to integrating nonfiction reading into your daily instruction across the curriculum. Careful choice of texts allows you to reinforce topics and skills through a variety of contexts. For example, if you are studying animal habitats in science, you will want to choose a variety of nonfiction texts about animal habitats in your literacy block or language arts lessons. To further student understanding, you can integrate the topic into math by sorting and graphing different types of animals and their habitats. By selecting a topic that aligns with your curriculum and allows for integration, you will enhance student understanding and fit more learning into the school day with ease and efficiency.

How do you teach nonfiction to students who are just learning how to read? The answer is to model as much as possible. Young children are like sponges, and they will take in all you have to share. When you read a nonfiction text aloud to the students, talk as you examine the features in the text. Explain what the text is teaching you and how it is structured so that it is easier to understand.

MATERIALS

To prepare for teaching nonfiction, you must first find the appropriate materials. While choosing materials, you will determine the structure of the text and look for text access features to focus on. Once you choose a nonfiction text, you will be ready to begin planning your lesson. The following will provide you with a step-by-step guide as you get ready to explore nonfiction with your students.

Choosing Texts

Nonfiction text may be in the form of a book, poster, article, webpage, or chart. To choose the proper text, you must first decide on an instructional focus. Your instructional focus may include the unique characteristics of a particular text structure or a focus on particular access features. Another example of a skill focus can be related to gaining knowledge on a particular topic. If you determine your instructional focus ahead of time, choosing texts will be easier. Also, consider that you will be using the same text for more than one lesson, so you want to be able to use the text you choose for a variety of instructional focuses.

Keep in mind that nonfiction material is presented differently than fiction material through the use of text structures and text access features. Students need to learn how to navigate nonfiction material by learning how to derive information from these structures and access features. It is important to choose materials that will enable you to highlight one or two access features and model their use in the text.

Text structure may be taught through the use of graphic organizers. It is important that some of your lessons include the teaching of structure and text access features as an instructional focus. This chapter contains an overview of how to prepare for teaching nonfiction. More specific information, as well as examples of activities, is given in future chapters.

Surround the students with nonfiction texts about topics you are working on in class. Find various resources, such as books, magazines, and printouts from websites, and put them in a visible place in the classroom so that students may refer to them. Be sure to choose materials that are appropriate for your younger students. See the bibliography for school publishers.

BEFORE YOU PLAN

Before presenting a topic, make sure students are equipped with some background knowledge. You can facilitate student learning by doing the following:

- Access students background knowledge on the topic before presenting the material. If students have no background knowledge of the topic, you need to present a short read-aloud or some kind of information on the topic, such as video or Internet resources.
- Connect the topic to your previous teaching. Making connections will help establish purpose and enable students to grasp onto the concept more easily. Choose the model text based on a specific skill focus.
- Assign a purpose to the reading. What information are you hoping students learn from the text?

Helpful hint: Plan out a scope of sequence for how you will introduce each access feature. Some build on each other, such as heading and subheadings or captions and photographs.

PLANNING A LESSON

Once you have chosen your topic, text, and skill focus, you are ready to think about planning your lesson. Lessons for each type of text structure may vary, but the basic lesson format will remain consistent. When planning a lesson with nonfiction, you will plan your lesson using "before, during, and after" reading strategies. This design is used for both read-alouds and small group instruction.

The following will provide you with an overview on how to go about planning a lesson using nonfiction text. Specific examples are provided throughout the rest of the book.

Step 1

Choose a graphic organizer that aligns with the structure of your text. The graphic organizer helps students understand the structure of the text and how to organize text information. See the appendix for blackline graphic organizers or create your own.

Step 2

Choose key vocabulary to introduce and highlight as you read. We often hear the terms *Tier 1*, *Tier 2*, and *Tier 3* when referring to vocabulary instruction. Your instruction will focus on Tier 2 words. Tier 2 words are those that students use in a variety of contexts from the time they learn them. They are not common sight words (Tier 1) or technical terms (Tier 3). Tier 2 words need to be first taught explicitly and then practiced in a variety of contexts until they are mastered. They should be spiraled into future lessons across the curriculum to ensure that they become a permanent part of a child's usable word memory bank.

As you plan, think about how new vocabulary will integrate throughout the day in other subject and specialty areas. For example, the word *circumference* may be used in math, art, gym, and even on the playground. Find creative ways to use the words in different contexts so that students may internalize their meanings. Make time for students to play with the words—for example, have students create posters displaying their meanings.

Step 3

Choose one or two text access features to focus on. Students need to become familiar with how information is presented through these text access features. These are the features that differentiate between fiction and nonfiction and help build understanding. A text access feature "walk" is a wonderful preview activity to focus students on gaining meaning from the text.

Here is an example of a possible feature walk: "I see captions under each photograph that help me understand what is being presented" or "The heading before each section helps me understand what the focus of the text will be, and the subheadings help me know where to read if I need more information on a topic."

Step 4

Comprehension strategies that help students understand fiction material may also be applied to understanding nonfiction material. Choose one or two comprehension strategies to focus on as you prepare the lesson for the text. You will be modeling the use of comprehension strategies with nonfiction materials so that students can see how the same strategies used in fiction reading can connect to different types of texts. Comprehension strategies are referred to as *metacognitive processes* that a reader applies to gain meaning from text. The terms for these strategies can vary. We will use the terms *guessing/predicting, wondering, picturing, noticing,* and *figuring out* (Boyles 2004).

Model the use of comprehension strategies as you read to the students. For example, say to the students, "I see an elephant on the cover of this book. I predict that I may learn more about elephants as I read." "I notice that the author put a caption under this picture of the elephant. Let's read the caption to see what more we can learn." "This map helps me figure out where the elephant lives."

In summary, when you are planning a lesson for presenting a piece of nonfiction, do the following before reading the text to the students:

- Determine skill focus
- Choose an appropriate text with a clear structure and access features
- Build background knowledge
- Connect to prior teaching
- Choose a graphic organizer that illustrates the structure of the text
- Choose key vocabulary to introduce
- Focus on one or two text access features
- Choose one or two comprehension strategies to model

LESSON COMPONENTS

When you are teaching text structure, a lesson should contain the following:

Before reading: Model/think-aloud
During reading: Talk about the structure and access features
After reading: Replicate the structure using a graphic organizer or a short piece of writing

Before Reading: Modeling/Think-Aloud

Many publishers create nonfiction materials at early emergent reading levels so that students may experience reading many types of nonfiction text at their independent or instructional reading level. Lessons using read-alouds and small group instructional materials at various reading levels are shared in this book.

When modeling the structure, be sure to clearly define it to the students. Point out key words and phrases used in that structure as you read, and use a graphic organizer for further clarification. While previewing the piece, model your thought processes (think-aloud) as you use the structure to gain meaning. It is essential to point out why the book is a certain structure and how the structure type is organized. For example, when you choose a book to model with students, first determine if the text is fiction or nonfiction.

Think aloud with the students. "Let's look at this book. I wonder if it is fiction or nonfiction—how can we tell? Yes, Lindsay, we see real photographs on the cover. What do you notice as we look inside? Yes, Michael, we see pictures with captions, a map, and an index in this book. These are some of the features that we may find in nonfiction books. This particular book is going to give us lots of information about the rain forest. It is a description. Each page describes a different part of the rain forest. Can you tell me some of the things you notice about this book?"

During Reading: Talk about the Structure

The purpose of this part of the lesson is to encourage students to verbalize the why and how of the text structure. Begin by choosing short text, or break up longer text into smaller chunks so that students will not be overwhelmed. Then ask students questions that focus attention on particular aspects of the structure. "Does this book show us how to do something? Is this book describing something?"

Teachers should start at the listening level first so that students may attend directly to the structure. This step begins to shift responsibility for learning from the teacher to the students by guiding students to recognize key words and phrases and/or design in the piece.

Other critical talk points:

Key words. Teach students to recognize key words—or *signal words* (as described in chapter 2), also called *content vocabulary*—that identify text structures and help them organize and comprehend the text more easily. For example, if students hear the key words *materials* and *ingredients*, they should be able to determine that the text structure is procedural and that they will learn how to do something.

Teachers need to model with explicit think-alouds how key words help them recognize the structure of the text. When key words are recognized, accompanying graphic organizers can be chosen to enhance understanding.

Visuals and dialogue. Oral language is a major instructional strategy for building understanding in the younger grades—this is why modeling is key. However, it is important to move beyond modeling to engage students in critical thinking. Providing visuals and engaging students in dialogue will build deeper understanding. Dialogue can occur between teacher and students or from student to student.

Young readers benefit by teaching through the use of visuals, such as photographs, maps, charts, and graphs, which can build literal and inferential thinking skills. For example, provide students with a photograph that has enough detail for students to state the obvious and make inferences about what they see.

Engaging students. Differentiate questions based on students' oral language ability. Ask questions that require more than a *yes* or *no* answer, and encourage elaboration. Rather than ask, "Do you see —— in the picture?" ask, "What are the —— doing in the picture? What in the picture makes you think that?" Another way to elicit a response may be, "Tell me about this picture (chart, graph, etc.)" When sharing a nonfiction text, pause to share an access feature, such as a chart, graph, or map, and discuss the new information learned from it.

After Reading: Replicate the Structure Using a Graphic Organizer or Short Piece of Writing

Once students have gained some experience with identifying a particular text structure, they should be able to produce that structure on their own. This can be done individually, in groups, or as a whole class. Some activities for producing a type of text structure are a piece of writing, completing a graphic organizer, or creating a skeletal outline based on the text passage. Students should be encouraged to use key words and phrases characteristic to the structure in their writing. Producing a class book is an effective activity that can also be revisited over time for review.

Remember that when you are looking for a nonfiction book to go with your lesson focus, knowing the structure of the piece will enable you to choose the most effective vehicle for instruction. For example, if your goal is to have students create a science experiment, you would model with a procedural text. Table 3.1 explains each text structure's purpose and format and gives an example of how to link to content area learning. More information on how to determine the structure of a text and choose an accompanying graphic organizer is included in chapter 4.

Remember, when planning a lesson, it is important to preview the content and vocabulary in the text that will be presented. Also when planning your lesson, choose one or two access features so that you can provide a graphic organizer for the structure of the text. Your "before reading" activity with students may include a think-aloud to model your thinking as you preview the text with the students. Students may use prior knowledge and make connections to predict what they may learn from the text.

The "during reading" activity can be planned for either whole class or small group work. Vary instruction with the whole class by asking questions at many different levels. Differentiate small group instruction by

Table 3.1

Nonfiction Structure/Form	Purpose	Format/Characteristics	Learning Link
Descriptive Texts about a specific topic	To describe, to classify, to organize and record information	(a) Introduction of topic (b) Subtopics about subject (c) Conclusion	Science—students tell what they learned about a topic
Recount; collection Biography; specific event	A retelling of a person's life or an event	(a) Introduction: who, what, when, where, why (b) Series of events (c) Conclusion *Key words*: first, second, next, finally	Students create a timeline
Procedural Text containing recipes, experiments, directions, etc.	Directions on how to perform a task	(a) Background information (b) Various step-by-step activities (c) Conclusion *Key words*: materials, ingredients, first, next, then, numbered sequence	Students break down a task into specific steps: create poster or how-to book
Explanatory/ expository Texts about why things happen	To explain	(a) Introduction: questions (b) Explanation in sequence (c) Conclusion	Students research to answer their own "why" question

providing each group with a different task based on the students' ability. One group may read the text with the teacher, while other groups may read and record information independently or assume reciprocal reading roles.

After reading, build comprehension by connecting information learned to prior thinking. Apply the skills taught by organizing thinking with a graphic organizer that suits the structure of the text. Demonstrate learning by having students write in the same genre and apply the vocabulary learned to their writing. Learning can be assessed by asking focus questions and having students use access features to demonstrate their learning.

MAKING ROOM FOR INDEPENDENT READING

Sort Your Classroom Library Books

What should your classroom look like to allow for optimal exposure to teaching nonfiction structures? Begin by sorting the books in your classroom into fiction and nonfiction groups. Rather than physically locating the books in separate areas, try differentiating them with easy-to-see stickers. For example, you could use a particular color of star stickers for fiction, then choose a sticker of another shape, such as a circle, for nonfiction. Because you will be sorting your nonfiction books into text structure categories, you will need various colors of whatever shape you have chosen.

Your library may be sorted according to topic, reading level, interest, and so on. Start by sorting piles into fiction and nonfiction. Sticker the fiction titles and set aside.

Now, sort all of your nonfiction titles by text structure. Place a different colored circle sticker onto each type of text structure—for example, red for recount, purple for procedural, and green for descriptive. In the younger grades, you may only have samples of three or four text structures in your library.

After you complete placing colored stickers or shapes on the books in the children's library, begin to sort the big books, read-alouds, and reference books you share with the class, using the same sticker colors that you chose for the classroom library books.

Create a large chart to serve as a key for the colored stickers or shapes. Use picture clues for each structure indicated on the chart so that nonreaders can also use the chart as a resource. A sample chart is provided (table 3.2).

How to Choose a Just-Right Book

Now that your classroom library is set up, it is time to get the students ready to choose independent reading books. Setting up a book box to

Shape or Colored Sticker	Text Structure	Visual Clue
	Fiction	
	Nonfiction: Descriptive	
	Nonfiction: Recount	
	Nonfiction: Procedural	
	Nonfiction: Explanatory	

Table 3.2

store each student's current reading material is an effective way to foster independent reading. Book boxes can be purchased or specially made from cereal boxes.

To make simple book boxes, cut each box by measuring two inches up from the bottom and cutting on a diagonal line up to the top of the opposite corner. Once the boxes are cut, they can be covered with contact paper and decorated in a variety of ways. If students are able to make their own book boxes, be sure and make yours first to model how to create it. Then model how to choose just-right books to fill it. Note that books that are placed into the book boxes should mimic the genre variety included in the classroom library. Go to your classroom library and choose books for your own book box.

It is important to model how to choose a just-right book. Let the students see what you do when you choose a book. As you choose books, talk about what you are interested in reading about and why. Model for students how to choose a just-right book, asking and answering the following questions. Read a page aloud to the students and comment if you think the book is too hard or just right to put into your box.

Ask yourself out loud:

Do I like the cover?
Do the pictures seem interesting?
Are there enough pictures to help me understand?
Is the type in the book the right size?
Does this book seem okay for me to read by myself?

If the answers to these questions are *yes*, then you have a just-right book to put into your book box. Once the students start to choose their own books, check to make sure that they are picking books at the right level for them. If you notice them choosing books that are too hard, introduce them to the "three-finger rule." It is a great strategy to determine independent read-

What's in the book?	Like	Dislike
Do I like the cover?		
Are the pictures interesting?		
Are there enough pictures? #		
Is the font the right size? A A A		
Is the book okay for me to read by myself?		

Table 3.3

ability for young children. Include this information about the rule in your newsletter to parents so they can encourage independent reading at home:

1. Open to the middle of the book.
2. Read the words on the page.
3. For every word that is too hard, hold up one finger.
4. If you are holding up more than three fingers by the end of the page, the book is too hard.
5. If you are holding up fewer than three fingers, the book is just right.

When students begin to read books with more text at about the third-grade level, they may use the five-finger rule.

The following chart (table 3.3) may be displayed or placed into children's book boxes to help them choose books for independent reading.

Lesson Plan Templates

Table 3.4

Before Reading Graphic Organizer / Text Access Feature / Think-Aloud	During Reading	After Reading
Preview • Content • Vocabulary • Organization Predict	Set purpose (recognition) Read-aloud or Small groups	Build comprehension Apply the skill (production)
Connect to background knowledge Vocabulary: Comprehension skill: Text access feature(s) focus: Think-aloud (modeling)	Choose books at an appropriate level for each group 1. 2. 3. 4.	Demonstrate learning: Writing • Write in the same genre • Apply vocabulary to writing Access the learning • Ask questions that focus on content • Ask questions that enable students to refer to access features • Ask students to explain graphs, charts, maps, etc.

Linking Reading and Content Learning

Materials to build/activate background knowledge:

Teaching/learning connection:

Nonfiction Planning Template

Book Title: _____

Content Area: _____

Topic: _____

Before Reading
Background knowledge/prior teaching connection:
_____
_____

Vocabulary:
_____

Text Access Feature:
_____

Comprehension Skill:
_____

During Reading (Small Group)
Purpose:
_____

Group 1:
_____

Group 2:
_____

Group 3:
_____

After Reading
Questions that focus on content (enable students to use access features):
_____
_____

Writing assignment/activity to demonstrate learning:
_____

Four
"Before Reading"
Strategies

This chapter explains the many possible ways to introduce a nonfiction piece or unit to the class. It contains suggestions for the "before reading" portion of your lesson plan with students. "Before reading" strategies/ activities are defined in this chapter, such as using photographs, anticipation guides, RAN charts (reading and analyzing nonfiction), and introducing vocabulary.

DETERMINING THE STRUCTURE OF THE TEXT

How do you determine the structure of the text? In chapter 1, we introduced and defined each nonfiction text structure to help plan your lesson. When you choose a nonfiction text to use with your students, it is important to determine which text structure the book follows so that you can plan your lesson with graphic organizers and skills that align with the structure.

Each structure has a slightly different look to it and with practice, each will become easier to identify. One way to determine the structure is to determine what the purpose of the text is. Is it to describe something or to show how to do something? Is it a timeline of a person's life or a comparison between two or more things? Once you determine the purpose of the text, you are one step closer to determining its structure.

Table 4.1

Purpose/Question	Text Structure
Does the text tell about a specific topic?	Descriptive
Is the text a timeline of a person's life or specific event?	Recount
Does the text give directions on how to perform a task?	Procedural
Does the text explain why things happen?	Explanatory

Table 4.1 is a chart of questions you can ask and the structures they match. As you use this information to plan your lesson, you may also ask students the same questions and/or refer to this chart as a "before reading" strategy with your students.

Another way to determine the structure is to see which graphic organizer is the best match for the text (table 4.2). Which organizer enables you to sort the information presented in the text?

Noticing key words, or signal words as described in chapter 2, and ideas in the text is another way to determine the structure. A description will center on a topic. A recount uses words such as *first, second,* and *last,* which indicate a time order. A procedural text uses words such as *materials* and *ingredients* and may show a numbered sequence. An explanatory text may have many questions that get answered throughout the text and may appear as question/answer books.

As you can see, there are many ways to help determine the structure of a text. You can examine the purpose of the text, see how the information best fits into graphic organizers, and look for key words/signal words or ideas.

BUILDING AND ASSESSING BACKGROUND KNOWLEDGE

Building background knowledge is a key tool for enabling young students to make connections to new learning. Before reading, you should connect concepts to prior teaching to help students grasp the informa-

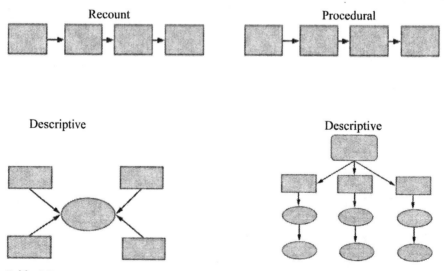

Table 4.2

tion more easily. One effective way to build background knowledge is through read-alouds. By listening to stories on various topics, students will store information and create a schema of knowledge to draw from when they are learning something new.

Another way to build background knowledge is through the use of web resources such as Discovery Learning, Google Earth, and other forms of video media. Students can actually see and experience real events or places through the use of web and video resources. If your school is able, planning field trips that align with nonfiction topics you are studying is also an effective way to build background knowledge.

Webbing is an effective tool to use when assessing background knowledge and building schema. To create a web, write your topic in a box. Branch off of the box with categories such as color, shape, size, where to find it, what it is like, what is it not like, and animal/plant/mineral. Your chart may look like table 4.3.

Topic lotto is a motivating activity that can be used with young children to help them build background knowledge. To create lotto boards, cut several magazine pictures or pieces of clip art pertaining to your topic. Be sure to make copies of each picture to use as caller cards. Paste six pictures randomly onto lotto cards for students to use. To play, hold up picture cards (caller cards) for the students. Students who have that picture will place a marker over the picture. The student who fills his or her lotto board first is the winner. Table 4.4 is an example of a student lotto board for insects.

Class discussion is another effective strategy for building background knowledge. Allow students to ask questions about topics that were discovered in the story. Have them help one another answer questions by sharing connections they have to the topic. Discuss how the new information is related to something they had previously learned.

You may also explore other resources on that topic to find new information. For example, always have a large map handy. When students

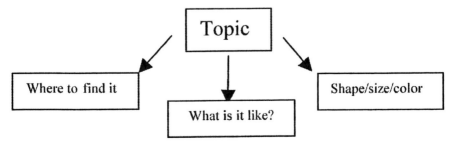

Table 4.3

are learning a new concept that is tied to a specific location, such as the Amazon rain forest or a specific animal species, it is helpful to show them where the rain forest is located or where the animal species lives. Try to integrate technology as much as possible by using Internet resources or classroom software to provide more information on a topic.

Photographs and Visuals

Photographs are a wonderful resource for building students' literal and inferential comprehension skills. As students preview the text before reading, they will develop skills such as finding facts and supporting details, comparing and contrasting, noticing the setting, summarizing, inferring, questioning, and predicting. Photographs allow for higher-level thinking that would normally be presented in text that is too difficult for young learners to read. Children can think and comprehend at much higher levels than they can read.

Here is an example of using a photograph to develop nonfiction comprehension skills. This activity is adapted from Tony Stead's book *Reality Checks* (2006).

1. Present a photograph that has enough detail for students to state the obvious and make inferences (table 4.5).

2. Ask students to state obvious facts about the photograph. Have them point to the details in the picture that prove their stated facts. If a student gives a fact that is not supported by the picture, such as "That is

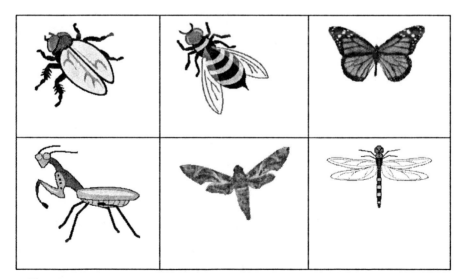

Table 4.4

Table 4.5

Table 4.6

Facts	Questions	Inferences	I think that because . . .
There are three elephants.	Is this an elephant family?	The elephants are thirsty.	The elephants look like they are getting ready to drink from the water, and I know
The elephants are in the water.	Are the elephants going to take a bath?		that animals need water to live.
There is one baby elephant.	How long does the baby stay with its mother?	Elephant families stay together.	I see a baby elephant with two larger elephants.
There are trees in the background.	Where do elephants live?	Elephants need water and trees where they live.	The elephants are standing in water and I see trees in the background.
		All elephants have tusks.	All three elephants in the picture have tusks.

an elephant family," put the statement in the form of a question in the question column.

3. Examine the photograph more closely and encourage student to make inferences about what they see. This will tap their background knowledge on the topic and make them use details from the photograph

to support their thinking. When a student provides an inference, ask, "What do you already know that makes you think that?" or "What in the picture makes you think that?"

4. Record all student responses on a chart or smart board. Refer back to this chart as you study more on the topic. Add new facts in a different color as students gain more information (table 4.6).

Anticipation Guides

Write important details you wish to have students recall onto a chart (table 4.7).

The teacher reads each statement to the students. The students write their name on a sticky note and place it in the column they believe it should go. After reading, students move their sticky to a different column if their knowledge of the statement changes. Each statement is reviewed, and evidence from the text is used to prove or disprove each statement.

RAN: Reading and Analyzing Nonfiction

The RAN strategy (Stead 2006) may be used in conjunction with a chapter in a textbook, a nonfiction picture book, a nonfiction leveled book, an article, or any other piece of nonfiction.

1. Have students write three things they know about the topic.
   a. Have students circle one of the three things and write it on a sticky note. (For younger grades, the teacher may write the facts on the sticky notes.)
   b. Post the sticky notes onto the "What We Think We Know" portion of the RAN chart. (You may use a smart board instead of a paper chart and sticky notes.)
2. Read the text to the students, or have students read it.
3. Have students move the sticky notes to the column "Yes, We Were Right" only if the fact was directly stated in the text. Facts may be revised if they were close.

Table 4.7

Statement	True	False	Unsure
An insect has four legs.			
A spider is an insect.			
An insect has three body parts.			
All insects have wings.			
There are more insects than people on Earth.			

Table 4.8

What we think we know	Yes, we were right!	New facts	Wonderings

4. Read the text again. Add new learning into the column labeled "New Facts." Once students become familiar with the process, add a new column, "Wonderings."
5. Add new facts the students wonder about onto the chart.
6. Students may research to find new information.

You may laminate a large RAN chart (table 4.8) to use over and over again or use a smart board for this activity.

INTRODUCING KEY VOCABULARY

It is essential to preteach key vocabulary before reading a nonfiction selection so that students can make sense of the information while reading. A simple way to introduce new vocabulary is for the teacher to choose six or seven new words from the text through an oral language activity.

For this activity, say one word to the students and provide an example of how that word is used in context within the text. Then provide the students with a definition of that word. After the definition is given, provide another example of the word in child-friendly terms. Have the students repeat the word at least three times, then think of his or her own example of the word. Ask students to share their examples with a partner. Give students a couple minutes to discuss the new word with their partner, then have students share the example their partner used.

The teacher may then point out any special characteristics of the word—a familiar chunk, multiple meaning, a special beginning or ending that was studied, and so on. Pointing out special characteristics of the word helps to connect it to prior teaching.

Repeat this process for each word you choose to introduce. Students need multiple exposures to new words to retain them. Allow students to have multiple exposures to new words throughout the day, and then continue to integrate these words in future lessons.

Word Walls and Family Word Journals

Build a home-school connection by having each student create a family word journal. When you introduce new words, have the students illustrate definitions for their words, then bring their journals home to share with their families. Have each student work with his/her family to create new illustrations to show how the words were used, or can be used, in other contexts.

Allow time for students to share their family word journal with the class—a word show-and-tell. Photocopy some of the new word illustrations to post on an illustrated "word wall." Continue to build and review the word wall throughout the year. Use words from this word wall to teach chunks, prefixes, suffixes, endings, and phonetic skills. This will enable students to constantly revisit terms introduced throughout the year. Use the words in various contexts, not just during science or social studies instruction.

Mystery Box

When building background knowledge or introducing key vocabulary, it is helpful for students to use concrete objects. Young children are more able to make connections and grasp onto learning more easily through the use of concrete objects. Build background knowledge with a "mystery box" activity. Mystery and suspense will engage this age group and help maintain focus. This activity may be used intermittently to get students curious about the topic of discussion.

- Begin by singing to the tune of "London Bridge": "What is in the box today, box today, box today? What is in the box today? Let's find out."
- Next, give a hint—animals, plants, and so on.
- Tell them how many objects are in the box.
- Have the students choose objects and predict what the topic of learning will be.
- To reinforce vocabulary, write the item names on chart paper as they are chosen.
- Give the function as well as the name.
- Pass the objects in a circle when they are all out so that all students have a chance to have their hands on them.

This may be used again as an "after reading" activity.

Mystery Poster

Obtain a poster that displays your topic.

- Cover the poster with large paper so the students are not able to see any of the poster. This may be done on a bulletin board.

- Gather students around the mystery poster.
- Have students guess what they think is on the poster.
- Tear off a small piece of the cover paper and have students make more predictions.
- Continue to tear off small pieces of cover paper and have students make predictions until they guess what is on the poster.
- Activate prior knowledge by asking students what they know about the topic the poster displays. Give students time to share and have a discussion about what they know.
- Provide each student with a paper that contains boxes or a piece of paper folded into sections. Have students draw or write words that pertain to the topic in each box on the paper.
- Have students meet with partners to share the words on their grids.
- After students have shared with partners, have each pair share three words from their grids. Have the class discuss the words and how they relate to the topic.

Mystery Poster Session 2

- Gather students around the poster.
- Ask students questions that lead them toward using words related to the topic shared in the previous lesson.
- Share websites with the students that continue to build background knowledge.
- As students share words that are relevant to the lesson, write these words on sticky notes and put them onto the poster.
- During the lesson, pause to ask students to clarify the words or act them out. Ask questions in order to help students clarify words.
- After words are clarified, break students up into small groups. These should be heterogeneous groups, including students of various needs and abilities. Each group should select one of the words from a sticky note and then decide how they want to present the word to the class. They may write out an explanation, act out the word, illustrate it, or share examples they find in the books you have assembled.
- Have each group present its word to the class and discuss the definitions. Record definitions on sticky notes and add them to words on the poster.

Silly Sentences: Before/During/After Activity

- Write new vocabulary words on chart paper.
- Read each word to the students.

- Have students work in pairs or small groups to make up sentences using words from the chart.
- Have each group share its sentences. Record all sentences on chart paper.
- After reading the text, discuss the meaning of each word on the chart.
- Read the made-up sentences.
- Determine which sentences make sense according to the actual meaning and which are "silly sentences."
- Refer to the text to make the silly sentences into sentences that make sense according to the meaning of the words as used in the text.

Illustrating Words

- Choose six to eight words from the text. These should include words that students will use in a variety of contexts (Tier 2), as well as technical terms that students will need to know to comprehend the text (Tier 3).
- Give a student-friendly definition.
- Read the passage from the text where the word occurs.
- Teacher creates a sentence with the word and shares with the class.
- Provide each student with a blank paper to draw on.
- Divide the paper into six to eight squares.
- Dictate each word and have the students illustrate each word in a corresponding square.

Word Web

A word web (table 4.9 and 4.10) is a good instructional strategy for introducing new vocabulary as well as accessing background knowledge on a topic. Word webs may be done with words or pictures. Try to model vocabulary by bringing in concrete objects. If you have a book about weather, bring in an umbrella to talk about a rainy day.

Develop oral language by modeling sentences using your prop—for example, "I like to carry an umbrella on rainy days. I wear my snow boots and mittens on snowy days." Let the students take turns with the props and talk about what they how they use the props in reference to the topic. After students have practiced the new vocabulary with concrete examples, you can move onto using the vocabulary words in the word web. Younger students will need picture cues included in the web.

Supply your students with pictures pertaining to your topic. For this example, we are going to use the sample book *Weather and Seasons*, published by National Geographic. Students may use these pictures to brainstorm words for the web. Students may then match pictures to the

Table 4.9

Helpful hint: Save magazine and calendar pictures to use for modeling vocabulary and topic information. Hold on to objects that may be used as props for vocabulary.

words on the web. This will help differentiate the lesson to meet the needs of the students in your class. Some students may read the words, while others may need to use the picture cues.

To extend this activity, provide students with several pictures of different kinds of weather. Students may sort each type of weather into columns under each key word. To integrate writing, students may dictate or write brief sentences to accompany each picture—for instance, "A rainy day. I like to fly my kite on a windy day."

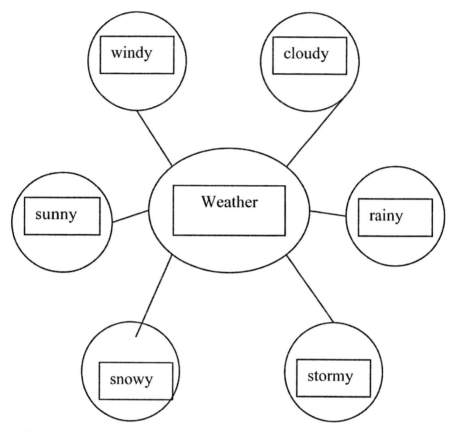

Table 4.10

Helpful hint: The computer program Inspiration/Kidspiration is a fun way for students to create information sorts and webs. Student-created PowerPoints engage.

LEARNING TEXT ACCESS FEATURES

Fiction and nonfiction texts have features that enable students to learn more about the story/topic and acquire information more easily. In fiction, some of these features include illustrations and dialogue. In nonfiction, several features help to organize and present information, such as table of contents, chapter headings, and photographs. These features help readers locate information more easily, organize information, and further understand the information.

Through teacher modeling and think-alouds, students become familiar with the use and purpose of text access features, which help them fully comprehend nonfiction text. Before you read to the students, point out some access features included in the text. Explain how the features help you better understand the information in the text, and share examples of access features in text.

Let's say one of your focus access features is a diagram, and you have been studying insects in class. Ask the students, "What information is the diagram showing us?" "How does this diagram make it easier for us to understand the information?" Explain to the students that the diagram is an organizer that presents information more clearly.

When we read nonfiction texts, many access features help us understand the presented information more easily, such as diagrams. Model the use of one or two access features as you share the text with the students. After reading, have students share how the access features helped them better understand the information (table 4.11).

You may differentiate your teaching while introducing text features to the students. The less mature students will need the most teacher guidance. For this group, you will model the text feature by writing the name of the feature on the board and posting specific examples. Students may look through the text and find examples that correspond with the models you posted on the board. Typical learners can work in small groups to find the focus features in their text. Mature learners may work with a partner to sketch examples of the focus features and/or find examples of the feature in multiple books.

A complete list of text access features is located in chapter 1.

MODELING COMPREHENSION STRATEGIES

Students need to be taught comprehension skills explicitly. In other words, comprehension strategies need to be introduced by the teacher, and students need various exposures with modeled and guided practice before they can use the strategies independently. Explicit teaching includes the gradual release of responsibility, in which the teacher scaffolds instruction until students can become independent.

It is important to remember that comprehension strategies are fluid and need to move throughout the entire lesson. Although these particular strategies are introduced before reading, they inherently continue as the lesson progresses. So please note that some of these examples given also include "during" and "after" reading application.

Following are sample models of how to introduce each strategy. The independent practice activities may be done in a whole class or small group setting, in the circle with the class, or at the students' own seats.

Table 4.11

Text Access Feature	What Is It? Describe It!	How Does This Help? How Do You Use It?
Table	An arrangement of information or data into columns and rows or a condensed list.	Good as a reference or a way to present data in a clear fashion.
Chart	A diagram or table displaying detailed information.	Good as a reference, a summary, or a way to comprehend or sort information in a clear fashion.
Key	An explanatory list of the symbols or abbreviations used on a map or diagram.	Gives understanding to the author's message.
Legend	An explanation of the symbols used on a map.	Helps the reader interpret the information.
Measurement	The size, length, quantity, or rate of something that has been measured.	Helps the reader get a perspective on the actual size an author is trying to convey.
Cartoon	Drawings with captions that may be published in a book or magazine.	Entertains and hooks the reader.
Cross section	A piece cut out of an object so that the inside may be viewed.	Helps the reader get a visual of the inside of something he or she may not be able to see in a concrete fashion.
Cutaway	A cross section or a part of a book or page that is cut away to show the information in more detail.	See cross section.
Inset	Something inserted into a larger picture, for example, a small map in the corner of a larger map.	This can put an enlargement in perspective to the whole for better reader understanding.
Font	Style and size of type.	Varies to keep the reader's attention or to emphasize or deemphasize a point the author is trying to make.
Sidebar	A short news story or a list of facts containing supplementary information that is printed alongside a featured text.	Gives the reader another way he or she may connect to the text.
Overlay	A transparent sheet containing additional details that is placed over a picture.	This allows the reader to add or take away detail for clarity and understanding.
Statistical box	Elements of data in a collection related to the topic or concept.	Helps the reader by presenting information that could be more confusing as a narrative or that is placed alongside a narrative for clarity.
Map	A diagrammatical drawing of something, such as a route or area.	Helpful for giving the reader a reference point.
Comparison	The process of examining two or more people or things to discover similarities and differences between them.	Shows the reader another way to interpret the text.

Guessing/Predicting

Purpose. To generate ideas about what may be learned in the text.

Model. Share the cover and title of the text with the students. Share your predictions of what you think may be learned in the text. Explain to the students that it is okay if their predictions do not match what is actually learned. By predicting, they will be able to remember what is learned in the text because they will compare how their guesses are the same as or different from what was learned.

Guided practice. Read the text aloud and stop at a point that allows for predictions. Have students work with you to give predictions.

Independent practice. Continue to stop at points in the text that allow for predictions. Have students give predictions independently.

Questioning/Wondering

Purpose. To generate questions to gain information from the text. Asking and answering questions helps you understand what you read.

Model. Read a page of the text aloud. Take time to pause as you read to generate questions. Come up with one or two questions that you thought of while reading that page. Explain that good readers ask questions as they read to help them pay attention to what they are reading and better understand. Write the questions on a chart for reference.

Guided practice. Read another page aloud. Ask students to work with a partner to generate questions to add to the chart. You may assist in helping students generate questions.

Independent practice. Students may be given the opportunity to generate their own questions after you read a page aloud. This activity may be done orally, or students may be provided with a white board to write out questions or draw picture cues as questions.

Inferring also falls under the guessing/wondering strategy. Good readers ask what information might be missing; then they guess what it is. Tell students that while reading, they should make a good guess to help them understand, based on what they know.

What does the story say?
What do you know that the story does not say?
Put the information together to make an inference.

Picturing

Purpose. To put a picture in the reader's mind to help better understand the text, using the five senses.

Model. Read part of the text aloud. Model using your five senses to create a picture in your mind. Draw a picture of what you've imagined. Explain to students that putting pictures in your mind will help you remember and better understand what you read and that it is okay for readers to have different pictures to help them understand. Be sure to include colors, perspective ("Are you looking at your picture from above or straight on?"), sizes of objects, and background.

Guided practice. Read part of the text aloud. Have students draw pictures on a chart of what they see in their minds. Prompt students to help them create a clear picture.

Independent practice. Have students draw pictures of what they see in their minds after you have read part of the text aloud. Provide students with smaller paper (e.g., 8.5 × 11 in.), so they have less space to fill and can add more detail.

> Put a picture in your mind.
> Read the text.
> Think about something in the text. What does it look like, sound like, feel like, smell like?
> Make a picture in your mind.

Noticing

Purpose. To see what the author put on the page (such as charts, pictures, diagrams, bold print) to help the reader understand the text; to help the reader determine what is important and monitor comprehension.

Model. Open the text to a page that has clear access features—a photograph, a chart, bold print, or something similar. Tell the students that you noticed the author used this component to help you better understand what is being taught in the text. Determine the most important information gained from the text.

Guided practice. Open to a page with clear access features and ask students what they notice on the page that helps them better understand the information. Coach them as they point out access features. Guide students to share what important information was learned from the text.

Independent practice. Have students look through the pages of the text and point out what features the author used to help the reader better understand the information. Have them write important information that was learned.

To monitor understanding:

> Go back and reread.
> Do the pictures or access features help you to understand?

Read on. See if the answer comes to you.
Ask for help.

Figuring Out

Purpose. To understand what the author was trying to say. Summarizing is a skill within this strategy.

Model. Share the table of contents with the students. Explain that you can figure out what you will be learning in the book by seeing the titles of each section. For example, the table of contents might say, "Where polar bears live; what polar bears eat." You can tell the students that you figured out that you will be learning about polar bears—where they live and what they eat. You may also model this strategy by reading a page aloud that answers a question you have or the class has. Explain that you were able to figure out the answer to your question after reading the information on that page. Text access features, such as headings and bold print, are also good models for figuring out. Model how to write a summary based on the important information that was learned. Writing a summary involves telling important ideas in your own words.

Guided practice. This strategy is best practiced during and after reading. As you read the book to the students, coach students to notice when they have figured out the answer to a question or when a text access feature has helped them figure out information. Have students tell what was learned after each chunk of text.

Independent practice. Have students use pictures to tell or write about what they learned from the text. Another option is to provide them with a graphic organizer to complete.

MORE COMPLEX STRATEGIES

Identifying the structures of cause/effect or compare/contrast within a nonfiction text can be difficult to young readers because nonfiction tends to lack cohesions, such as *because, so, however,* and *unlike,* which can signal a cause/effect or compare/contrast relationship. Even when texts do contain these cohesive ties, students may be unsure how to use them to connect ideas and gain meaning. Students will need guidance to recognize these relationships and comprehend texts that contain these structures.

Identifying cause/effect relationships is a strategy readers use to figure out why things happen. A cause is what makes something happen, while an effect is what happens. For example, heavy rain causes flooding. You may model cause/effect by using a graphic organizer (table 4.12).

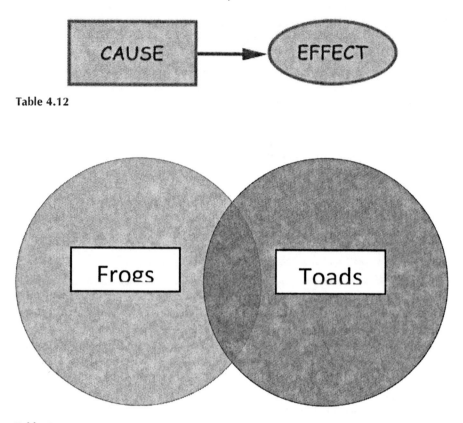

Table 4.12

Table 4.13

Comparing and contrasting is also an effective strategy to use for building comprehension. Compare things to tell how they are alike, and contrast to tell how things are different. For example, students may have learned about frogs and toads. To compare/contrast these two animals, students will need to apply the information that was learned from the topic. Organize ideas by using comparison circles (table 4.13). Concepts that are different will be recorded in each circle, while concepts that are the same will be recorded where the circles overlap.

Background Knowledge for Comprehension

Young students depend on background knowledge for linking new learning. Before reading, it is important to build and assess background knowledge so that any misconceptions that students have about a topic can be clarified before they start making connections to inaccurate information. In doing this, also link newly introduced vocabulary to students' background knowledge.

The text access features chosen and introduced add another layer of learning and are then comprehended using a focus strategy. Careful planning before lesson presentation is essential to maximize student learning, as young learners' primary learning occurs within the first fifteen minutes.

Building Comprehension Before Reading

Have students preview the book before reading. They may look at the front and back covers of the book to predict what the book will be about. Then read the table of contents with the students. Ask if any of the chapter headings or subheadings give them clues about what they might learn in the book. Help students generate questions about what they may learn in the book. Questions should be recorded on a chart (table 4.14) so that students may record answers to their questions after reading. Here is an example of a table of contents chart from the book *It's about Time*, published by the Wright Group.

Creating a chart like this one encourages students to monitor their reading by giving them a purpose. As you read aloud or the students read, they will seek answers to their questions within the context of the text and through the text access features. After reading, students may fill in the answer to their questions. They may even note what access features helped them clearly answer their questions.

Another type of chart includes chapter headings and subheadings. Each heading and subheading are the chapter title and subtitle included in the table of contents. Here is another example based on the book *It's about Time*.

SQ3R Strategy

Students have to learn how to interact with the text rather than just reading it. One of the easiest ways to do this is to use SQ3R (table 4.15), a tech-

Table 4.14

Chapter Heading Clue	Question	Answer	Access Feature Clue
Time across the World	How can I tell what time it is in other parts of the world?		
Telling the Time	Are there different ways to tell time? What are they?		
Telling Time Today and Beyond Time Machines	Do time machines really exist?		

Table 4.15

There's Something about Mondays		
Just How Long Is a Day?	Never-ending Long Weekends	What a Difference a Year Makes

↓

Time across the World
Why Back-to-Back Birthdays?

↓

Telling the Time		
Shadow Time	Water Clocks	Sand Time

↓

Using Weights and Springs	
You Better Watch It	A Pendulum Did the Trick

↓

Telling Time Today and Beyond
Time Machines

nique frequently taught in elementary and middle school. For younger learners, this technique can be done with teacher guidance.

Each letter in SQ3R stands for a separate step:

S: Survey the material by previewing all the headings and subheadings.
Q: Write a question for each heading. This gives students a purpose for reading and/or listening carefully.
R1: Read the material under a heading and find the answer to the question created in the previous step.
R2: Restate the answer aloud to reinforce material.
R3: Students review the previous steps.

Survey
Heading:_____

Question: _____

Reading (answer to question)

_____

Restate Answer

Review

Before Reading Planner

Name of Text:_____   Topic: _____

Text Structure: descriptive   recount   procedural   explanatory

Background Knowledge:

_____

Teaching Connection/Focus:

_____

Graphic Organizer:

Key Vocabulary Words:

_____   _____   _____   _____

_____   _____   _____   _____

FIVE

"DURING READING" STRATEGIES

Helpful hint: The computer program Inspiration/Kidspiration is a fun way for students to create information sorts and webs. Student-created PowerPoints engage.

Up to this point, this book has explained how to prepare a lesson that includes a topic, text, vocabulary instruction, and purpose/instructional focus. Now, it is time to read the text. This chapter shows you how to maintain the focus of the lesson purpose by keeping the students engaged in learning. Ways to differentiate the lesson to meet the needs of all students are explained.

MODEL TEXT

A model text is the book, article, passage, magazine, or piece of nonfiction work that you use to teach with. You will use the model text in several lessons to teach nonfiction elements such as text structure and text access features, as well as topic content.

Plan your stopping points ahead of time. Your stopping points will be based on the text access features you are teaching. Even though the author may have used many text access features in the book, you will want to be specific about what you are teaching. Your teaching should be specific, planned, and explicit. As you read to the students, stop and explain how the features help you better understand the information in the text.

Think aloud as you read through the model text. Your think-aloud will include commenting on how the access features help you further understand the information, noticing vocabulary in context, and explaining how applying comprehension strategies helps you gain meaning. Here is an sample think-aloud that uses a model text about dogs. Note how the comprehension strategies are woven through this think-aloud. It is important to maintain consistent language when teaching and modeling comprehension strategies.

Sample Think-Aloud: Access Features

- I am noticing that the heading for this part is "Helping Dogs." I am guessing that I will learn about different types of helping dogs in this part of the book.
- I am noticing that the captions under each photograph are telling me about different types of people and professions that use helping dogs. I wonder how the dog in this picture is helping.
- I am noticing that the dog in this photograph has a special harness and that the person with him is relying on this dog to cross the street safely. I am guessing that this person may be blind, so I am figuring out that this is a seeing-eye dog.
- Now, let's read more of the text to see if my predictions are correct.

There is no need to model every feature used in the text, just the features you choose to focus on. When you introduce more features in future lessons, you may refer back to the model text. Let your students watch as you model the use of chosen access features while you work through the text. As you read, some students will begin to copy your model and begin to interact with you and the text. This will give meaning to access features, and it is a good way to see who will need to have more supported instruction in small groups and who will be able to work more independently.

After you read, ask students to reflect on how those features helped you learn more about what was being presented. The turn-and-talk procedure is an effective strategy to engage students.

> The turn-and-talk procedure is when students talk with a partner to think aloud or practice a strategy based on the directive given by the teacher.

Following the think-aloud as described in the "Helping Dogs" model, you would tell the class something like "I read about a special kind of dog. What kind of dog? Yes! Helping dogs. Turn and talk to your partner about the ways dogs are helpers." Differentiate based on student responses and interactions with the text as you read to the students.

During your think-aloud, focus on vocabulary in context. Text features, such as charts and diagrams, will help highlight key vocabulary concepts. As you read the text to the students, stop at intervals to ask questions, elicit discussion, and teach more words at point of use. Use gestures, pictures of real objects, and quick draws to further explain what a word

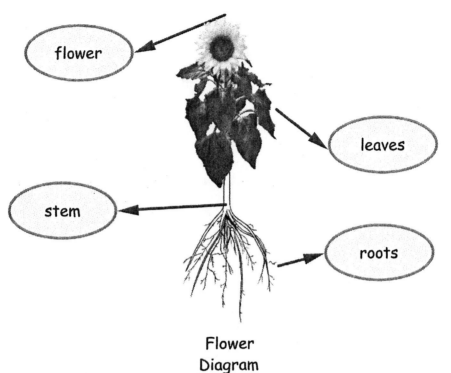

Flower
Diagram

Table 5.1

Emerging learner: The student who will begin to remember, understand, and apply information presented with more than appropriate grade-level instruction and continual guidance or prompting; the student who will not be independently able to follow through with lesson requirements.

Typical learner: The student who will remember, understand, and apply information presented with appropriate grade-level instruction and guidance; the student who will follow through with the lesson requirements.

Mature learner: The student who will remember, understand, apply, analyze, evaluate, and generate additional ideas with the same appropriate grade-level instruction and minimal guidance; the student who will take your information and independently apply it across environments without additional instruction.

means. Making the words more concrete will help young students grasp their meanings.

If you are reading a book about insects, some key vocabulary that may have been introduced before reading can include *thorax, abdomen,* and *antennae.* As you read, have students point to these body parts in the pictures. Stop periodically and ask them to tell you what body parts insects have. Show pictures of other bugs and ask them to tell you if it is an insect or not and why. These reinforcements will help students remember the key vocabulary that was introduced prior to the lesson.

You may differentiate as you work through the text to meet the needs of all the learners in your classroom—for example, when looking at a diagram such as table 5.1.

With emerging learners, read the vocabulary words in the diagram out loud slowly and have them repeat the words after you as you point to them in the diagram. Have some students come up to the text and point to each part of the plant as you say the word. For typical learners, put students into groups of two or three and have them give a sentence about each part of the plant, such as "The stem holds up the leaves and flower." For mature learners, display a picture of a plant. Have students work in pairs to label each part of the plant and give a sentence about each part of the plant.

Using a chart or graphic organizer as you read the model text will help students focus on the purpose of your lesson. Graphic organizers, such as comparison circles and main idea/detail charts that correspond with each text type, are included in the appendix. What follows is sample read-aloud text, followed by a chart (table 5.2) that can be used as a tool for modeling the importance of text access features. (A blank copy of the chart is also included in the appendix.) With young students, it is best to fill out this chart together as you read the think-aloud text to the students. As you read the model text aloud, fill out the chart with the students.

Sample Think-Aloud: Chart as Tool

- Here is a photograph and caption on page 8. Those are two of our focus features. Let's put them on our chart.
- The word "Photograph" goes into our "Feature" column.
- Let's write "page 8" in the "Page Number" column so we can find it again if we need to.
- Now let's describe the feature in the next column. "This is a picture of a dog with a red vest that has pockets and reflectors. The dog is not on a leash, and there are several people watching from a mountain of snow."
- Now think about how this text access feature, a photograph, helps us to understand better about what the author is trying to teach us

in this text. With a photograph, the author shows us the details he wants us to see, so we don't have to create a picture in our mind. We can actually see the red vest and where the reflectors are on it and how the dog walks along with the guide and doesn't run ahead. We can now fill in the last column. This picture shows me how the dog can do more than the people. This looks like a type of rescue dog.

Book title: *Dogs*
Focus Features: Headings, captions, photographs
Name: Zitnay Miner

Feature	Page Number	Describe It!	How Does This Help?
Heading	3	There are words before the paragraph that tell what the paragraph will be about. The heading says, "Helping Dogs."	This tells me what this part of the book will be about. I know I will learn about helping dogs. This tells me what I will learn about.
Photograph	4	This is a picture of a dog with a special harness and a person holding onto him to cross the street. A picture of a dog helping a person.	This gives me another way to learn the information besides just reading the text. The picture shows me a type of helping dog. This dog is helping a blind person cross the street. This shows me more about the topic.
Photograph	8	This is a picture of a dog with a red vest that has pockets and reflectors. The dog is not on a leash, and there are several people watching from a mountain of snow. The dog is wearing a red vest.	This picture shows me how the dog can do more than the people. This looks like a type of rescue dog. This shows me more about the topic.
Caption	8	The words under the picture tell that the dog is a special kind of rescue dog who can sniff out and search for people trapped in an avalanche. The words tell about the picture.	This tells me what the dog is doing in the picture, so I understand what the picture means. This tells about the picture.

Helpful hint: You may fill out each column or only the first three columns during reading and then have the students fill out the final column as an "after reading" activity. This chart may also be used for independent or small group work.

To keep students on task and give them a purpose for reading, a shape sheet is an engaging activity. Choose shapes that match your topic. For example, you may use animal shapes, flowers, fruits and vegetables, vehicles, or weather icons. As students read, have them write facts into each shape on the sheet. This may also be used as the teacher is doing a think-aloud. With clear stopping points predetermined in the lesson plan, the chart can be filled by the teacher and students together.

Facts about the Solar System
By _____

Write a fact or concept that you have learned inside each shape as you are reading.

More mature learners may do this activity independently, in pairs, or in small groups. Emerging students may draw pictures or write single words in the shapes. For these learners, provide them with an organizer that is partially filled in. Provide page numbers so that students can easily locate the information that is needed to complete the organizer. The previous page shows an example of a sheet to use while reading about the solar system.

If you had used a RAN chart prior to reading (see chapter 4), you will stop throughout the text to confirm or revise facts that were shared by the students and add new facts as they are encountered in the text. Many facts may not be confirmed during reading, and students may generate questions based on what they are learning. These questions may be added to the "Wonderings" column as you read.

Sample RAN Chart

What We Think We Know	Yes, We Were Right!	New Facts	Wonderings

If you had used a KWL (know/want/learn) chart prior to reading, we recommend that you also revise any inaccurate prior knowledge that was given. Young children hold onto background knowledge as a means of connecting new learning. If their prior knowledge is inaccurate, new learning will also be skewed. The following is a sample of a modified KWL chart that may be used to confirm or revise prior knowledge as you read.

Sample KWL Chart

What I Know		What I Want to Know	What I Learned
Confirmed	Revised		

DIFFERENTIATED SMALL GROUP INSTRUCTION

The following are formats that may be found in your classroom.

Independent Readers

Independent readers are self-directed students who are able to work with minimal instruction.
Appropriate activities for these students include the following:

- Creating questions and answers based on information gained in the text
- Listing questions that they have after reading text that was unclear
- Listing questions that go beyond the information in the text and researching the answers
- Recording difficult words and research definitions
- Filling out a graphic organizer based on text structure
- Reading a book at their level and filling in an access feature chart
- Taking notes in their content area notebook as they read so they may complete their entry after reading

Supported Readers

Supported readers read at their instructional level with the teacher.
Appropriate activities for these students include the following:

- Reading in sections with teacher direction
- Pausing to consider questions after completing each section (these may be a combination of student- and teacher-generated questions)
- Monitoring comprehension while reading—with the teacher continuing to use the think-aloud process until students begin to demonstrate automaticity with strategies
- Focusing on text access features to gain understanding
- Working with a graphic organizer based on text structure

Reciprocal Reading Role Players

These students read independent text while adhering to the structure of the reciprocal reading model. This format may be started as early as second grade.
Appropriate activities for these students include the following:

- Predicting, creating questions, clarifying, and summarizing

- Making predictions based on cover, back cover, title page, and table of contents
- Generating questions that can be answered by using the text and text access features
- Seeking information to confirm/revise predictions
- Clarifying information that is unclear or includes difficult vocabulary
- Summarizing the text using graphic organizers and/or content notebooks (Oczkus 2003)

RECIPROCAL READING AS A STRATEGY

Reciprocal reading roles consist of predicting, questioning, clarifying, and summarizing. Apply these strategies when organizing activities with students. Use of reciprocal reading has proved effective in student acquisition of comprehension (Marzano 2004). Here are some examples of how you can incorporate reciprocal reading into the early elementary classroom.

Predicting

- Preview the front and back covers and text access features (illustrations, headings, charts).
- Note vocabulary and phrases pertaining to the topic.
- Predict what is likely to be learned based on clues from text access features.
- Apply what students know about the topic to help make a prediction.
- Modify predictions as the students proceed through the text.

Students may use the following language while predicting:

- I think . . . because . . .
- I'll bet . . . because . . .
- I wonder if . . . because . . .
- I imagine . . . because . . .
- I suppose . . . because . . .
- I predict . . . because . . . (Mowery 1995)

Questioning

- Ask questions based on the text access features (captions, sidebars, photographs, charts, etc.).

- Ask questions based on the topic of the reading.
- Ask some questions based on text structure (cause/effect, fact/opinion, main idea/detail).
- Ask questions that require investigation.

Question words and phrases include the following: *who, what, what if, when, where, where else, how did, how else, how would, how could, why, why else, why would,* and *why could.*

Clarifying

- Note confusing ideas associated with the topic.
- Point out introduced text access features and how they convey information.
- Identify Tier 3 words that are unknown or difficult to understand.

Clarifying phrases:

- I didn't understand the part about . . . , so I . . .
- This doesn't make sense, so I should . . .
- I can't figure out . . . , so I should . . .

Clarifying strategies:

- Reread, reread, reread.
- Read on for clues.
- Check text access features.
- Compare with predictions.
- Relate to prior knowledge.
- Discuss with group.

Summarizing

- Retell key points or ideas.
- Leave out unnecessary details.
- Summarize in logical order dependent upon text structure.
- Reread parts of the text for the main idea.
- Review text access features to retell or summarize the text.

Summarizing phrases:

- The most important ideas in the text are . . .
- This reminds me of . . .

- This topic is important because . . .
- The text features show us . . .

In summary, as you read nonfiction text, you will apply comprehension strategies and notice how text access features help you understand the information presented. You will model your thinking aloud for the students, then scaffold by gradually letting the students tell about what they are learning from the text. You will ask questions that require students to refer to the text or access features within the text. Avoid simple *yes* or *no* questions. Reinforce the use of comprehension strategies, such as noticing and wondering as you read.

"During Reading" Planner

Name of Text: _____   Topic: _____

Text Structure: descriptive   recount   procedural   explanatory

Stopping places:

wPg. _____ for _____   wPg. _____ for _____

wPg. _____ for _____   wPg. _____ for _____

wPg. _____ for _____   wPg. _____ for _____

wPg. _____ for _____   wPg. _____ for _____

Teaching Connection/Focus

_____

_____

Key Vocabulary Words

_____   _____   _____   _____
_____   _____   _____   _____

Graphic Organizer
Chart: Procedure: Web:

Topic/details: Shape specific:

Text Access Features

table of contents   headings   glossary   diagram   chart

captions   bold print   photographs

Comprehension Strategy

predicting   connecting   picturing   wondering   noticing   figuring out

Assess for Understanding

Turn and talk

Riddles / Clues
1.
2.
3.

Six
"After Reading" Strategies

This chapter highlights skill application techniques such as building comprehension and applying, demonstrating, and accessing learning. Once you have modeled your lesson and students have completed reading the text, it is time to build comprehension and apply learning.

BUILD COMPREHENSION

An effective way to help students connect is to use a graphic organizer. The KWL chart in this chapter helps the children pinpoint what they think they know before reading and helps clear misconceptions after. Any time you activate prior knowledge, be sure to check for accuracy.

COMPARISON CIRCLE ORGANIZER

Compare information learned from a previously read text on the same topic to the information in the current text.

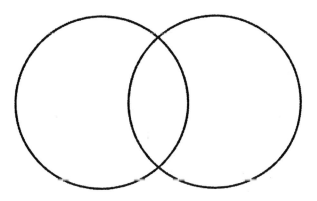

KWL CHART

Add new information that the students learned from the text. Be sure to refer to text access features throughout the book when adding new learning to the chart. Remember, it is important to confirm or revise students' background knowledge as you work through text so students can connect new learning to accurate information. After reading, use the KWL as a resource for nonfiction writing. Students may write a few short sentences or a short paragraph about what they learned.

MODIFIED KWL CHART

What I Know		What I Want to Know	What I Learned
Confirmed	Revised		

APPLY THE SKILL

Complete a graphic organizer based on text structure (see appendix). Then use text access features to summarize or explain the content:

- The photographs showed me . . .
- When I looked at the maps, I learned . . .
- The index helped me predict . . .
- The diagram helped me understand . . .

DEMONSTRATE LEARNING

- Practice key vocabulary words in other contexts.
- Extend the topic by writing a piece in the same genre as the text.
  - For example, write a how-to (procedural) book or article; write a comparison about two topics; or write a description about the topic.
- Journal writing:
  - My first reaction to the topic . . .
  - Surprising new information . . .

Page #	New Information

- o Something I already knew . . .
- o Something I learned more about . . .
- o Questions I still have . . .
- o If I were to present this topic to the class, I would say . . .
- o This connects to my previous learning because . . .
- Create pictures, charts, diagrams

ACCESS LEARNING

- *Questions:* Ask questions that focus on content.
  - o Literal questions that focus on topic and details learned
  - o Inferential questions that force students to refer to access features to answer the question
  - o Content and structure questions that allow students to focus on the text structure—cause/effect, procedural
  - o Questions that allow students to ponder author's purpose and background
  - o Ask students to explain graphs, charts, maps, and so on.
  - o Ask questions that make connections between evidence and explanations.
  - o Ask questions that will allow students to understand that scientific explanations have models and theories that support them.
  - o Ask questions that allow students to reflect on why people respond differently to changes in culture and environment.
- *Notebooks:* Students may keep a content notebook for each area of the curriculum—science, social studies, math. Science notebooks are very effective in the younger grades. Students record information using pictures and labels. Content area notebooks allow students to learn note-taking skills in the context of the classroom. These notebooks can be used to help students do the following:

Comparing spiders

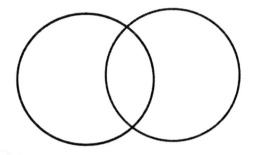

- o Make sense of their understandings by using recording and organizing strategies that are personally meaningful. Students may create charts and diagrams based on access features found in the text. They may also write descriptions or draw pictures of what was learned in the text.
- o Teachers assess content area notebooks by giving "quizzes" on the content. Students may use their notebook as a reference while taking the quiz. The grades on the quizzes will reflect the effectiveness of the students' notebooks. Teachers may gear note-taking lessons based on the quiz grades.
- o After the quiz, students may reflect on how to take better notes.
- *Puzzle share:* Have each group share what they learned about their topic to the class. Encourage groups to take notes as each group shares information on their topic.

SAMPLE WRITING LESSON

Students can use the same structure as the text in their writing. For example, if the text had a descriptive structure using main idea/detail, students may use the main idea/supporting detail structure in their writing. Students may use graphic organizers to assist in their writing. The following prewriting organizer may be used for the main idea/supporting detail structure.

1. Model how to brainstorm using the graphic organizer. Let's refer to the book about insects. Write the word *insects* on the topic line.

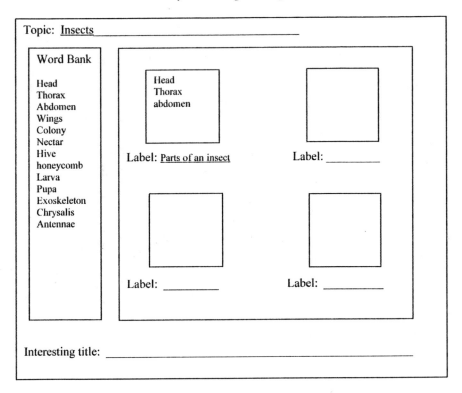

Topic: Insects

Word Bank

Head
Thorax
Abdomen
Wings
Colony
Nectar
Hive
honeycomb
Larva
Pupa
Exoskeleton
Chrysalis
Antennae

Head
Thorax
abdomen

Label: Parts of an insect

Label: _____

Label: _____

Label: _____

Interesting title: _____

Think of some words related to insects and show students how to write these words in the "Word Bank" column. Prompt students to think of words about insects—they may refer to the bold words or glossary. (This is another way to get students to use text access features.) Add the words the students generate to the list.

2. Model how to group the words. Find three or four words in the word bank that go together in some way. Write them inside one of the boxes. Think of a label that sums up why these words go together. For example, *head, abdomen,* and *thorax* may go together and be labeled "Parts of an insect."

3. Help students group the remaining words.

4. Challenge students to think of additional words for each group. They may use background knowledge or seek other resources.

5. Show the two ways that this organizer can help them with their writing.

   a. The labels can be headings or chapters. Then the words can be the main ideas for the paragraphs.

   b. Each label could be a main idea for a paragraph. Then the words can the supporting details within each paragraph.

6. Compare and contrast the completed outline with the chapters and main ideas in the book. Explain that there are different ways to write informational reports—share reports from the students.
7. Teachers may differentiate by having students complete this activity independently, in pairs, or in small groups. Some students may need to work in small groups with the teacher.
8. It is important to have each student/group share his or her report and to encourage other students to ask questions. Sharing and class discussions help increase vocabulary and oral language skills, which in turn enhance comprehension skills.

APPLY THE STRATEGY

Allow students to use the word bank blackline master included in the appendix to create an informational report about a different topic. They may choose a different animal or topic than what they have studied in class. When completed, have them think of an interesting title for their report.

After reading, students need to apply what they have learned. They should be able to refer back to the text access features in the book to demonstrate their learning. Look back at our weather word web in chapter 4. A suggested activity was to have students sort pictures of each type of weather according to the key words: *windy*, *sunny*, and so on. After reading, students have gained more knowledge about each type of weather.

An example of this would be the introduction of seasons within the book. Different types of weather occur during different seasons of the year. A picture diagram is used to show the seasons in the book. To access learning, provide students with the pictures of the different types of weather. Rather than sort the pictures by types of weather (sunny, windy), have the students refer to the diagram in the book and sort the types of weather by season.

This activity will require students to refer to the seasons diagram in the book to match the types of weather with the appropriate season. It will also help the teacher gear instruction by showing which students understood the content and were able to use the access features in the book to find information.

Helpful hint: Have students create poems or songs related to the topic. They will need to follow a model (see appendix).

To the tune of "Are You Sleeping":

Leaves are starting; leaves are starting,	Then comes fall, then comes fall
In the spring, in the spring	when leaves turn, all colors
The leaves begin as buds	red, orange, gold, and brown
Then they open up,	then they fall all over town
See them grow, see them grow	See them fall, see them fall
Leaves are growing; leaves are growing	Leaves in winter, leaves in winter
Making shade, making shade	hide inside, hide inside
The leaves are all done growing	They stay inside the tree
And leaves will keep on showing	Where we can't see
All summer long, all summer long	saying warm, staying warm

Haiku:

> Leaves are new in spring
> Making shade in the summer
> Change colors in fall

Shape organizers make nonfiction summaries fun. Using the topic of discussion—spiders, for example—copy each body part on a different color paper.

- Provide each student with parts to create a complete spider.
- Have students put a fact about spiders on each leg.
- Write a thesis statement in the head.
- Write a descriptive paragraph on the body.
- *Option:* Each body part could be designated for habitat, food, types, prey, and so on.

Other ideas for a shape organizer include parts of a flower, mammals, body systems, electricity, insects, and so on; for social studies, covered wagons, ships (explorers), and maps.

Connections improve student comprehension and retention of information. Using the Internet or print materials, have students find connections about the topic. For example, if students are studying a particular animal, they may find other places in the world where that animal lives or where other animals are similar, including zoos as well as natural habitats.

- An example for biology-related studies—places where the animal or insect is found.

- An example for physical sciences could be other experiments done by the same scientist or other discoveries that came out of the original discovery.
- If students are studying an explorer, they may list a food product from each place the explorer went. The class can also collect or prepare recipes from these places. This can even evolve into a whole cultural study unit culminating with a fair in which each student is responsible for a project on his or her country or region.
- A class survey lets the students see if a member has visited any place the explorer went or if any student has family that originated in a particular country or region.
- For students to make personal connections, relate the topic to the five senses—for example, fall, "I taste fresh apples," "I see colorful leaves," "I smell wet leaves," "I feel the wind," "I hear the leaves crunching."

These connections can be demonstrated in different writing genres.

- Facts can be listed, displayed on a poster, written as a report, or put into a book format.
- Cartoons can be summative of information or give a snapshot of an event in a person's life.
- Persuasive pieces or commercials can be written to promote scientific discoveries or explain why a new invention will help life.
- Students can pretend they are the person being studied. The students can then write journal entries or letters to friends, relatives, or pertinent people from that person's perspective, giving accurate facts. For example, being Columbus, they can write to the queen of Spain persuading her to give him money or even detailing weather, the morale of the crew, what the journey was like, discoveries, and how they will help Spain.

3-2-1 chart: Students fill this out individually, with a partner, or in a small group. To begin, the teacher models with a think-aloud: "After I read about spiders, I learned that they are not all poisonous. I am going to write that down. I also learned that some spiders can jump. I will write that down. Hmmm, I know! Spiders can help get rid of harmful insects. Now I need to write down what I connected with. The book said that spiders live in all kinds of neighborhoods—I see spiders in my neighborhood! I also connected with a picture of a spider—the picture looked like a spider I saw camping with my family. Ok, there is one question I still have after reading this book: How many kinds of spiders live in my state? I am going to write that down so I can look it up later."
Here is an example of a 3-2-1 chart:

3 Things I Learned	2 Things I Connected With	1 Question I Still Have
• Not all spiders are poisonous. • Some spiders can jump. • Spiders get rid of harmful insects.	• I see spiders in my neighborhood. • A picture in the book looked like a spider I saw when I was camping.	• How many kinds of spiders live in my state?

Have students create text access features that could be included in the book but were not, such as tables, charts, cross sections, or diagrams using the information from the text to complete the task. For example, students may create a diagram of a pet after studying types of animals or after introducing the text access feature diagram.

An activity to reinforce the understanding of text access features after a lesson may include using the following chart. Have students choose two to three access features found in the text. After the features, have them explain what the feature is and how it helped them further understand the information presented in the text. The teacher can act as a scribe for this activity in small group or whole class. Advanced students may be able to do this activity without much teacher guidance. This activity may also be done on a chart that can be displayed in the classroom.

Mystery poster "after reading" activity:

- After reading and learning about the topic depicted on the poster, have students envision themselves in the poster. Ask students to generate a list of phrases that relate to their experience in the poster. Encourage students to use topic-related words that they had learned in their reading material.
- Have students add more relevant words to the poster.
- Ask students questions about their experience. Questions should allow students to use information learned from the text.
- Have students add three to five words from the poster to their personal writing dictionaries.
- Have students write a piece about their experience in the structure of the text. Students may refer to words on the poster and in their personal writing dictionaries. Younger students may create an illustrated story or poster rather than a written piece.
- Have students share their stories/posters with the class.
- After all students have shared, have a class discussion about what was learned.

Text Access Features	What Is It? Describe It!	How Does This Help? How Do You Use It?
Glossary		
Index		
Table of contents		
Headings		
Subheadings		
Activities		
Connections		
Facts		
Diagrams		
Captions		
Photographs		
Illustrations		
Labels		
Bullets (dot points)		
Tables		
Charts		
Keys		
Legends		
Measurements		
Cartoons		
Cross section		
Cutaways		
Insets		
Fonts		
Sidebar		
Overlay		
Statistical box		
Maps		
Comparison		

- What was something surprising you learned about . . . ?
- What is something you will never forget?
- What is your favorite new word you learned and why?
- How was your first write different from your final write?
- What questions do you still have about . . . ?

Extension: Write words from the sticky notes onto index cards. Have students illustrate the cards. Place the cards into a literacy center so students may continue to practice them. Students may sort and categorize the words in the literacy center.

SEVEN

TEACHING NONFICTION
THROUGH TEXT STRUCTURES

Descriptive texts are most common in the younger grades. These texts center on one topic and are structured in a main idea/detail format. Many descriptive texts contain pictures with captions, drawings, table of contents, sidebars, headings, and subheadings.

You will model the use of comprehension strategies throughout your lesson so that students learn how to apply these strategies to their own learning. The following is a sample lesson using a descriptive text about insects.

DESCRIPTIVE STRUCTURE: BEFORE READING

Before reading a descriptive text, it is important to assess students' background knowledge on the topic. If students make connections to inaccurate background knowledge, new learning may be skewed. To assess background knowledge, you may use a RAN chart, KWL chart, web, or other graphic organizer. If you choose to use a KWL chart, be sure to make sure that inaccurate knowledge is revised before it is recorded onto the KWL chart.

An anticipation guide is also an effective way to assess background knowledge as well as provide focus to your lesson. Samples of some graphic organizers are given here. Full-page blackline masters are provided in the appendix.

RAN Chart

What I Think I Know	Yes, I Was Right!	New Facts	Wonderings

1. Ask students what they think they know about the topic.
   a. Mature learners may write their facts onto sticky notes.
   b. Beginning learners may dictate facts for you to write onto the sticky notes.
2. Post the facts students think they know onto the chart.
3. Review these facts as a class before reading, and explain that as you read, you may confirm some of these facts and move them into the next column.
4. Explain to the students that if a fact is not confirmed by the text, you will revise the fact to make it accurate before it can be moved into the next column. Some facts may require further research before they can be moved.

KWL Chart

What I Know	What I Want to Know	What I Learned

Modified KWL Chart

What I Know		What I Want to Know	What I Learned
Confirmed	Revised		

1. Ask students what they know about the topic. Scribe what students know into the chart, or write statements onto sticky notes to post onto the chart.
2. Ask students what they would like to learn from reading the text. Scribe student responses into the chart.
3. Explain that while reading, you will check the chart to see if any questions from the "What I Want to Know" column are answered.

Anticipation Guide

Statement	True	False	Unsure

1. Teacher writes three to five facts that she or he wants students to remember onto the anticipation guide before it is presented to the students. Some of these facts may be stated accurately, while others are changed to be inaccurate.
2. Let the students know that you will read each statement to them and that they will decide if they think the statement is true, false, or unsure.
3. Read each fact aloud. Have students place a sticky note with their name into the column of their choice.
4. Let the students know that after reading the text, they will have the opportunity to move their sticky note to a different column as they gain new information.

Topic Web

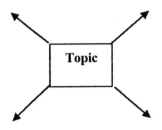

1. Write the main topic of the text into the center box.
2. Have students call out facts they know about the topic.
3. Write the facts around the topic box.
4. If students name several facts, you may create subheadings for your web and sort the facts.

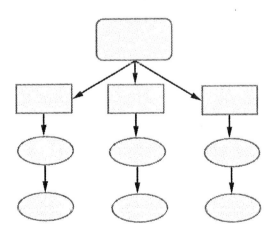

Before reading, it is important to introduce key vocabulary words to the students so they comprehend what these words mean as you read the text. You may do this by sharing illustrations of the words, creating a word web, or doing any of the activities described in chapter 4. You will also choose one or two access features to focus on and introduce these features to the students before reading. Remind students that they will notice these features within the text and that each has a special way of helping students learn and remember information.

The following "before reading" activities are based on the book *Insects*, by Newbridge Publishing.

1. Show the front cover and back cover to the students. Ask students to make predictions. What do you think this book will be about? Is this a story or nonfiction? What makes you think that? What questions do you think this book will answer?

2. Introduce a graphic organizer that matches the text structure. We will use a main idea/supporting detail chart as an example. This organizer will support a descriptive structure. Guide students to refer to the table of contents to complete this graphic organizer. This will emphasize the importance of text access features. Also, tap into students background knowledge: What do we know about insects? What different kinds of insects do we see at home or at school? Specifics may be added to each subtopic after reading the text.

3. Introduce key vocabulary. Some technical terms used in this book include *larva*, *pupa*, *metamorphosis*, and *colony*. This particular book has a glossary of terms that refer to insects. You would not introduce

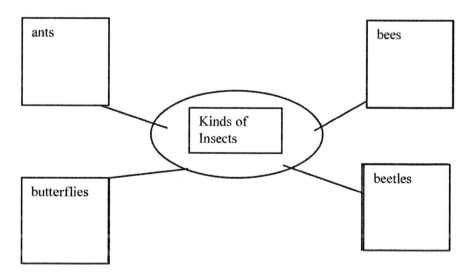

these words in one lesson. This book would be taught over a series of several days. Choose vocabulary words that match the chunk of text you will work with each day. For example, the first chapter is entitled "What Is an Insect?" For this chapter, you would introduce the words *thorax*, *abdomen*, *antennae*, and *exoskeleton*.

When teaching key vocabulary to young children, it is best to provide pictures, objects, or concrete examples. For example, you may show an actual or humanmade insect or a labeled chart to explain each part of the insect.

4. Text access features to focus on in this book are bold print, captions, and diagrams. The table of contents, glossary, and index should be reviewed for almost every lesson so that students are very familiar with using these features to gain information, as they appear in virtually all nonfiction texts. When reviewing the table of contents, ask the students, how does the table of contents help us guess what we may learn in this book? How can we use the table of contents to find information? What pages might tell me about butterflies? Take a look at the glossary. What are some new words we will learn in this book? Refer to the index. What pages can I go to learn more about butterflies?

When introducing new text access features, share an example and explain how it helps you better understand what is being presented in the text. For example, open to the diagram of the butterfly on page 8. This diagram shows me a picture of a butterfly. Each part of the butterfly is labeled—head, thorax, abdomen, wing, antennae—so I can see

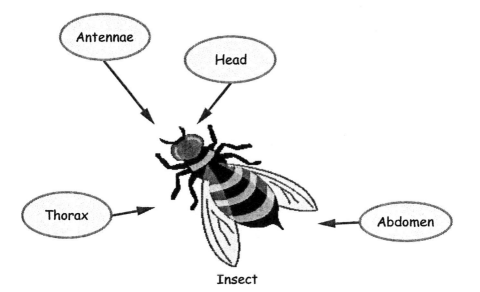

Insect

exactly what each part of the insect looks like and where it is. This helps
me better understand what the author is teaching me in this book.
5. Model how the same comprehension strategies you use to understand
   fiction can also help you understand nonfiction. "Noticing" and "figuring out" strategies will help students focus on text access features as
   they read. I am noticing that the author put a diagram on page 8 to help
   me to better understand/figure out what the parts of the insect are.

DESCRIPTIVE: DURING READING

During reading, it is important to focus on the facts that are learned about
the topic. Students will prove or disprove the information that was shared
prior to reading. New facts will be learned while reading, and new questions may arise. You will refer to the graphic organizer that was started
before reading the text to adjust prior knowledge and record new learning.

RAN Chart

What I Think I Know	Yes, I Was Right!	New Facts	Wonderings

1. Before reading, students recorded facts they thought they knew
   about the topic.
2. During reading, have students move their facts into the "Yes, I Was
   Right!" column.
3. If a fact was inaccurate, revise the fact so that it may be moved into
   the next column.
4. Record new facts into the third column while reading the text.
5. Be sure to refer to text access features, such as charts, diagrams, captions, and so on, to complete the RAN chart.

Modified KWL Chart

What I Know		What I Want to Know	What I Learned
Confirmed	Revised		

If you had used a KWL chart, confirm or revise the statements that students shared prior to reading. If you had written statements on a sticky note, you may use a modified KWL chart. Otherwise, you may use a different-colored pen to make revisions on your KWL chart.

Invite students to interact with the text as you read. Students may point out text access features and tell how the feature helps them understand the information. You may also create your own text feature, such as a chart or diagram, while you read the text as a way to take notes about the information. You may refer to the table of contents to create a graphic organizer for note taking.

If you had used a topic web before reading, expand on the web by adding additional facts. This is also a form of note taking.

As you read, model that nonfiction texts do not have to be read from beginning to end as fiction texts do. Descriptive texts are perfect for modeling this aspect of nonfiction. Read the table of contents to the students and ask them what they are most interested in. Refer to the index to locate information that may confirm prior knowledge that was shared before reading. Explore the book with the students, and study some of the charts and diagrams within the book to see what information is gained from them. Some texts may be too wordy for very young readers, so you may just read bits and pieces of a text during a lesson.

Let's refer to a book about insects for our supported readers group. During reading, remember your focus skills. We had chosen to focus on descriptive text structure and use a graphic organizer that utilizes main idea and supporting details.

Helpful hint: Small group instruction is an effective way to differentiate your teaching as students learn to apply nonfiction reading strategies at their level. Emerging readers require more teacher guidance, while mature learners may be able to read some of the text independently.

1. Open to the first chapter, "What Is an Insect?" Write the main idea, "insect," into the graphic organizer. Think aloud as you read the first paragraph to model main idea and details. This paragraph was mostly about insects having three body parts. The main idea is "Insects have three body parts. These body parts are the head, thorax, and abdomen." These body parts are the details that support the main idea, insects. Create a graphic organizer that corresponds with the information given in the chapter. Complete the graphic organizer with the students. A sample referring to a possible chapter on insects is as follows:

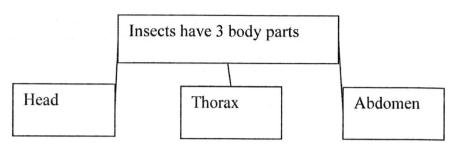

2. Continue reading the rest of the page. What main idea did you find in the next paragraph? To differentiate for students that need support, phrase your next question appropriately: The main idea in the first paragraph was insects have three body parts, because all of the text talked about insects having three body parts. Joey said the next main idea is the head because all of the text tells about the . . . ? Yes! Head. Now let's read the next paragraph. Read. In this paragraph all of the text talked about the thorax, so the main idea of this paragraph is . . . ? Yes! The thorax. Notice how the main idea words were in bold print. Bold print helps us learn new words as well as identify main or supporting details. Bold print words are usually followed by a definition or explanation of the word. This is the author's way of letting you know this word or concept is important. Refer to photographs and captions in the first chapter. Talk about how the captions enable you to gain more understanding about the topic. "The captions tell us what to look for in the picture."

3. Put students into leveled groups. With your mature learners, ask students to read the first page of the next chapter. Remind students to look at the photographs and read the captions because the photograph adds details to the text you might not be able to picture in your mind and the captions will help you focus your thoughts on the topic. If you come across any bold print words, write them down so we can talk about them. Tell students that when they are finished reading, they should list the main ideas in words or pictures, and you will talk about the main ideas and details they found on that page. Have your emerging learners illustrate the main ideas and list details for what was read previously. Meet with your typical learners to read the next section together, and then have them complete the assignment you had the mature learners do. Meet with your emerging learners next and complete the process together. If the mature learners complete the task, have them start on the next section. If you continue as a whole group because of your assessment of their proficiency, remind students, "As we read the first page of this

chapter, stop to look at the photograph and the caption under it because the photograph adds details to the text you might not be able
to picture in your mind and the captions will help you focus your
thoughts on the topic." Raise your hand if you come across any bold
print words so we can talk about them.

4. Observe and support students as they read. Offer prompts and guidance to students in need.

DESCRIPTIVE: AFTER READING

Remember, descriptive texts are centered on a main topic with supporting facts and details. There may also be subtopics within a descriptive
text. Children often have difficulty recalling facts, especially if the facts
are new learning or if there are many facts presented. After reading, new
learning, along with confirmed and revised facts from prior learning,
should be reviewed and expanded upon.

Refer back to the graphic organizer that was used before or during reading.
If you used a RAN chart, you will review all of the information on the chart.

What I Think I Know	Yes, I Was Right!	New Facts	Wonderings

Be sure to take time to talk about the revised facts that students had
shared before reading, and go back to the text to show where the information was found to revise the facts. Have students tell about the new facts
that were learned in the text, and go back into the text to show where the
new information was found. Encourage students to look back at text access features, such as captions, charts, and diagrams, to show where they
learned new information.

After reading, students may generate questions about their new
learning and be excited to learn more about the topic. Add the students
"wonderings" into the last column of the RAN chart. Make sure you find
time to do further research on the topic to answer students' questions.
You may find other books on the topic, search on the computer, visit the
library, or use web resources such as Discovery Learning.

If students filled out a KWL chart, they may complete the last column,
"What I Learned," after reading the text. Also review the confirmed and
revised facts and refer back to the text to find where the information was located. Read the questions students had shared in the "What I Want to Know"
column and highlight the questions that were answered and the information

in the "What I Learned" column that corresponds with each question. Have students refer to the text access features in the book that helped them to learn and understand this information. Circle the questions that were not answered in the text, and plan to do further research to answer these questions.

Remember, you do not have to read full texts to find answers to student questions. You may gather a few nonfiction texts and just refer to the index and table of contents to find information. This will model that nonfiction texts can be used a resource and do not always have to be read from beginning to end.

Modified KWL Chart

What I Know		What I Want to Know	What I Learned
Confirmed	Revised		

After reading, you may also review the key vocabulary words that were introduced prior to the lesson. Ask students questions that prompt them to refer to the key words—for example, "What three body parts does an insect have?" Students may refer to an insect diagram from the text or a word web that was shared prior to reading.

For a follow-up activity, encourage students to write. You will adjust the level of difficulty of this writing assignment according to the needs of your students. Young learners can draw and label a picture; other students may create a diagram or write a paragraph with a main idea topic and supporting details. Providing an organizer will help students organize information into a paragraph.

In reference to our book about insects, remember that our focus was the descriptive text structure, which mainly consists of main ideas and supporting details. We referred to the text access features of bold print, diagrams, and captions. For this book, you can focus on the text structure by asking, what have we learned about insects? What is each paragraph mostly about? What is the most important idea given in each paragraph? What details tell about the main idea?

- To focus on text access features, you can ask, how did the diagrams help you understand the parts of the insect? Where is each part located? How did the captions help you use the photographs?
- Also ask the students general questions that allow them to focus on the content. What did you learn that you didn't know before? What was the most interesting thing that you read? What do you want to find out next?
- Students may complete a main idea/supporting detail chart in reference to one of the chapters. This will allow the teacher to access the focus skills in the lesson. You may use a standard topic/main idea/detail chart like the one provided above, or you may draw your own. Draw a picture related to your topic and have students write a main idea and supporting details in each part of the picture. For example, if you are studying butterflies, students may write the main idea in the body and the supporting details in each part of the wings. Some students may still need support with this skill. Reteach and give further guidance to students until the skill is mastered.

Whole Class/Small Group

All activities listed here may be done with the whole class or in small groups. Publishers have recently added leveled nonfiction materials for young readers that do contain an appropriate amount of text access features to develop nonfiction comprehension skills in young children. When working with small groups, you may use manila file folders to make mini-RAN charts. Students can add sticky notes to the chart, and it may be saved for the group to work with on additional days.

RECOUNT STRUCTURE

Prereading with/Introducing Biography

A biography is a story of someone's life written by another person. An autobiography is a story of someone's life written by himself or herself.

A biography that is written as a story is much more interesting. Good
biographies keep the reader interested. Before introducing the structure
biography, building anticipation and connections is important. Students
need to feel that they can relate to someone else's story.

- Begin by taking out chart paper or an overhead with the heading
  "My favorite" or "I like." Have the students do what they love—talk
  about themselves!
- Some guiding questions to get the process started: Are you interested
  in sports? What do you watch on TV? What is your favorite song? Do
  you like to cook/bake? What do you play outside?
- When you have the list, start by saying, "Some of you said you like to
  skateboard. Do you know any famous skate boarders? Tony Hawk,
  good. Let's put his name by 'skateboarding' on the list." Another
  approach can be "I like to ride my bike. I wonder if there are any
  famous people who like to ride their bike. Oh! I know one—Lance
  Armstrong. Does any one know who he is?"
- If you or the students don't know a famous person, make a separate
  list and do a web search.

Helpful hint: There are many picture books about famous athletes, tele-
vision stars, and musicians, as well as illustrated chapter books. Ask
your school or local librarian to get them out ahead of time. If there are
not many titles, request that some be on the list with the next order.

Next take out biographical books you have previously collected that are
appropriate for the grade level in the different interest areas. As with any
of the other text structures, the most effective thing a teacher can do is use
the think-aloud strategy.

- "When I look through my book I see . . . " photographs, a timeline,
  table of contents, and so on. Talk about whatever the focus structure
  is or any that is in review.
- "Let's look through some of these books. Meet with your partner
  and I will give you a book to look at." Pass out a book to every two
  students and give them a topic of interest. "Go through the book like
  I did and talk to your partner about what you see." When choosing
  a biography on a particular person, focus on the person's main ac-
  complishments. For example, if the focus of the biography is art in a
  person's life, preview the work from that person. Compare/contrast
  other artists to this person's work.
- Create comparison circles for two different artists on what you observe before reading.

Although a recount mostly appears as a biography, we must remember that the structure of recount refers to a text that shows a series of events. A popular book for young readers that is an example of a recount that is not a biography is *Red Leaf, Yellow Leaf,* by Lois Elhert. This book shows the series of events from when a tree was born to when it was planted. The following lesson can be used before reading this recount:

1. Introduce the front and back covers.
2. Tap background knowledge—what do the students notice about the color/type of the leaves on the cover?
3. Show text access features in the book: pictures with captions, words with definitions.
4. Introduce key vocabulary: *leaves, buds, roots, sap, bark, seeds, tree flowers.*
5. Draw a large tree on a chart and have the students label the parts of the tree they know using the key vocabulary words.

Recount (Biography): During Reading

As you are reading, fill in a timeline of the presented facts. Due to the shorter length, most early elementary biographies focus on a major event, talent, or accomplishment in the person's life. One example is *Brett Favre,* by Richard J. Brennar (East End Publishing 1999). The author narrowed his topic, Brett Favre, to two pages about his birth date, birth place, and family. The rest of the thirty-two pages were related to football: pictures and football highlights in his life. As the books get lengthier, they can be taken chapter by chapter.

- A timeline can be presented as a list horizontally or vertically.
- It can be represented as any shape that is horizontal or vertical. For example, the Brett Favre timeline can be drawn like laces on a football.
- When reading aloud, fill in the organizer with dates and events from the person's life.

After modeling how to use a standard or shape timeline, have the students generate a shape that would represent something in the life of the person they are reading about. As they go along, students can fill in information with you on the timeline.

When you are reading,

- Point out that the author did not put every event in the person's life in the book.
- Note vocabulary words that are new.
- List important names in a chart organizer of friends, family, and other.

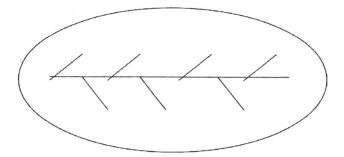

Football Timeline

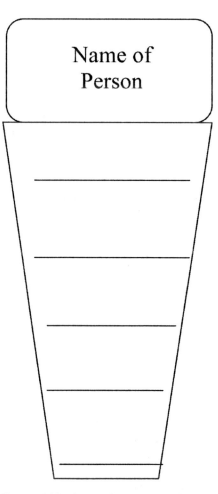

A famous singer's timeline could be featured on a microphone.

Mrs. Jones		
Friends	Family	Other People
Jean Smith	Mother	Reverend Hunt
Bob Happy	Father	Mr. Popular Teacher
	Mr. Jones	
	Sister Sally	

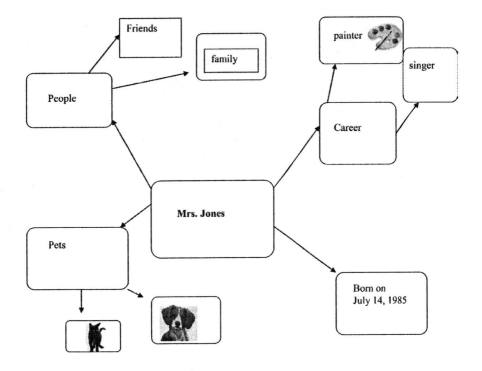

Draw webs of related information.

- When working on chart paper or an overhead, stop at headings and subheadings and draw a bubble to the central character's name and then detail bubbles after that.
- Pictures can be used instead of words.
- If you have access to a program such as Kidspiration, this can be used to model a custom web.
- This can also be done as an "after reading" activity

Helpful hint: An advanced student could be a friend of the character. Tell about things you may have done together. If you were a friend of Brett Favre, did you practice throwing the football to each other every day after school?

"After Reading" Biography

- If the biography you chose is an artist, have the students complete a project in the artist's style.
- Have students complete a timeline of their own life. Scaffold for emergent learners by the number of lines to fill in, or give them specifics of what to include (e.g., birthday, special toy, special vacation, first day of school).
- Pretend to interview the character. Generate a list of questions based on the kinds of things you read in other biographies, such as the following (questions can be added or deleted based on the level of the students):
  o When were you born?
  o Where were you born?
  o Who is in your family?
  o What is your favorite . . . ?
  o What made you choose to . . . ?
  o Tell me the most (surprising/interesting) thing that happened in your life.
- Be the character
  o Dress up as the character and report about yourself based on the above questions.
- Look at advertisements in magazines or product boxes and make your own.
  o Does the product match the person?
  o Does the ad make you want what the person is selling?
  o What might your person sell?
  o Does the person make you want to try the sport or craft he or she is famous for?
- Job application
  o Present the students with a job application and have them fill it in as if they were the famous person.
- Write biographies about classmates.
  o Use the sample interview questions to put together a report.
  o Students can present the biographies without telling the name of the person, and the classmates can figure out who it is. As an extension, students can use props and draw or take pictures to go along with the presentation.

o Put these into a class book.
- Students can write biographies about family members.
  o After the biographies are done and put in a published format, invite the subjects in to hear the stories presented. As an extension, students can use props and draw or take pictures to go along with the presentation.
- Famous animal biographies are another way to hook students into the idea of a life story.
- Another form for presenting is to create a diorama of an important time/scene in the person's life. Use an index card to write a paragraph describing what is shown and why it is important. (Be sure to have the student label the included people.)

After students study and create a modern biography, it is easier to relate biography to the subject you are studying.

- History—famous people in the period, such as George Washington and Martin Luther King Jr.
- Science—famous experimenters such as Galileo Galilei, if you are studying the telescope; John Glenn, when talking about space travel.
- Authors of the books being read—Eric Carle, Dr. Seuss.

PROCEDURAL STRUCTURE

The procedural structure follows a step-by-step format. This type of text may include how to make something, how to do something, or how something works. Lists and charts are common access features in procedural texts.

In addition to how-to books, recipes also follow the procedural format. Preparing recipes with students will not only enable them to become familiar with the procedural format but also help them build mathematical skills such as measuring.

Another way to expose your young learners to the procedural format is to post simple directions in the classroom. For example, if your students are doing a cut-and-paste activity, put the directions on a chart with picture clues. Make charts of simple directions and picture clues for several of the activities you do in the classroom. Laminate the charts so you can use them multiple times.

Before Reading

When introducing a procedural text, it is important to explain the purpose of this structure to the students. Explain that this type of text will

1.   Color

2.   Cut

3.   Paste

show them how to do something. Tell students that the author of a proce-dural text often uses photographs, lists of materials, and numbered steps to present information. When doing a procedure, it is important to follow the steps in order.

Some nonfiction text features that may appear in a procedural text are as follows:

Lists: Explain to the students that a list presents small pieces of infor-mation that may or may not be in a particular order. A list is easy to read and is used to help remember things. A list of materials helps the reader figure out what is needed to perform the task.

Charts: Explain that charts provide a way to present information in an easy-to-read format. Charts also make it easier to compare and contrast information.

Labels: Explain that labels identify specific parts or pieces of informa-tion in an illustration or diagram.

Glossary: Explain that selected words in the text are defined or ex-plained in an alphabetical list at the back of the book. This is called the glossary. Many texts that have words in the glossary appear in bold print throughout the text.

Numbered steps: Procedural texts often contain numbered steps to define what needs to be done to complete the task. Numbered steps provide an easy-read formula to readers in addition to, or rather than, an explanation in narrative form.

During Reading

A procedural text describes how to do something. Most procedural texts are formatted in a step-by-step fashion. While students are reading the text, guide them by asking them to make predictions before each step. "What do you think we will have to do after . . . ?" "What do you think the next step will be?"

Be sure to emphasize the text access features in the text. Charts and lists will be prevalent in procedural text.

- Model: "You can see the author used many charts and lists in this text. When you are going through a procedure or an experiment, it is important the steps and materials are clear so none are missed. Lists help organize materials so it is easy to understand; just like a grocery list, you know what you need. The chart will explain the process clearly and helps it stand out from the regular text so the reader will notice it."
- Ask students to use these features to explain the procedure as they read through the text.
- Model: "When you are reading, I want you to stop at a list or a chart and tell how it can help you understand your reading. For example, as I read this text on how water comes in three forms, I can stop and read the chart on how water changes from a solid ice to a liquid with heat, and I can see the list of materials I need to repeat this experiment:
  o Ice
  o Hair dryer
  o Cup"

The website www.sciencekidsathome.com has many experiments with household materials and simple instructions. Students can be put in heterogeneous groups to facilitate experiments after teacher demonstration.

Books about growing plants are easy to find at the primary level. How to grow pumpkins, beans, and fruit pits (stones) are all detailed in a step-by-step format. After reading one of these books, have students replicate the procedure for what was grown. A daily running record of plant progress in a sentence or two on chart paper will reinforce the vocabulary and what was learned. The procedures and records from each student can then be put into a class book.

For differentiation, and when students need a concrete way to understand procedural text, help them by scripting an everyday class activity. One example that can be shared is morning routine.

Model: "When we come into the classroom in the morning, what are some of the things we do?" Illicit student responses and list them on the board or chart paper. "Yes, we hang up our jackets, unpack our backpacks, put notes in the tray, take down our chairs, and start our seatwork. Let's write that as a procedure, or directions, in case anyone comes in and they don't know what to do. Let's start with 'First, come through the door.'"

Continue until the process is complete, slowly letting the students take over the wording and even some of the writing if appropriate.

1. Put away backpacks.
2. Give teacher notes.
3. Put homework in the homework tray.
4. Take attendance and lunch count.

After Reading: Procedural

Writing a procedure: Have students use what they have learned about procedural text to write a class book describing how to make something or do an experiment.

- Talk about possible topics to write about. Some examples may be various experiments in physical science, such as how batteries work, how magnets work, or sink/float. Topics may also include how to perform a task, such as how to grow a pumpkin, how to bake muffins, or how to make a craft. Scientific demonstrations may also be an option, such as how to determine wind direction, how to measure rain, and how ice melts fastest. Brainstorm ideas and then choose one to focus on. It is best to focus on topics the students have already learned about.
- Have students suggest materials needed to perform the task they chose. List the materials in a box under the heading "Materials Needed."
- Work with students to name each step involved in the task. Write each numbered step on a separate piece of paper.
- Distribute the pages to small groups of students, and have each group illustrate its step. Provide examples of procedural texts so that students may refer to the types of illustrations used in the texts.
- Bring the class together to share the steps and illustrations. As a whole group, write a page that summarizes the task.
- Create a cover for the book. Have students organize the pages in the correct order.
- Create a table of contents and glossary of terms.
- Once the book is completed and put together, have students take turns brining the book home to share with family members. After

everyone has had the opportunity to take the book home, keep the book in a book bin within the classroom so that students may continue to practice reading the book.
- You may also have students share the book with another class to assist them in performing the task in the book.

At the end of your unit, fill the mystery box with the objects from the current unit and any past units. Have students draw objects out of the mystery box and place them on the rug. Then, sort the objects into topics. (If the objects are from only one unit, they may be sorted into categories.) Students can also create their own boxes of pictures or objects to represent what they have learned.

Mystery Poster: "After Reading" Activity
- After reading and learning about the topic depicted on the poster, have students envision themselves in the poster. Ask students to generate a list of phrases that relate to their experience in the poster. Encourage students to use topic-related words that they had learned in their reading material.
- Have students add more relevant words to the poster.
- Ask students questions about their experience. Questions should allow students to use information learned from the text.
- Have students add three to five words from the poster to their personal writing dictionaries.
- Have students write a piece about their experience in the structure of the text. Students may refer to words on the poster and in their personal writing dictionaries. Younger students may create an illustrated story or poster rather than a written piece.
- Have students share their storied/posters with the class.
- After all students have shared, have a class discussion about what was learned.
  o What was something surprising you learned about . . . ?
  o What is something you will never forget?
  o What is your favorite new word you learned and why?
  o How was your first write different from your final write?
  o What questions do you still have about . . . ?

Extension: Write words from the sticky notes onto index cards. Have students illustrate the cards. Place the cards into a literacy center so students may continue to practice them. Students may sort and categorize the words in the literacy center.

EXPLANATORY STRUCTURE

This type of text is similar to the descriptive structure in that it centers on a topic, however, the format of an explanatory text is in the form of questions and answers about why things happen. Diagrams, headings, and subheadings are prevalent in the explanatory structure. The question-and-answer format is popular with elementary students. With this type of text, you want to focus on teaching headings and labels as the text access features.

The question-and-answer format is also useful for teaching predicting, as the prediction is confirmed or revised in the sentences that follow. Along with giving information, this question-and-answer format gives numerous examples in the use of what? where? when? why? and how? within questions. Children are repeatedly hearing and reading fluent questions that will enable them to stop and think when they are writing awkward or incomplete questions themselves.

In the book *How Does It Work? Questions and Answers about How Things Work,* by Jack Long, and illustrated by Vern McKissack, the author uses questions as headings along with labeled illustrations to present his information. Using the question "What happens to my food when I eat it?" assess for background knowledge about how much students know about the digestive system, and ask questions to elicit any specific details. You can draw an interactive diagram with any information the students give. Predict what else may happen when you eat. Then read the text to confirm or revise predictions. Complete the class diagram with information from the text.

A good follow-up activity is to take another piece of text, put it on chart paper, and read aloud a paragraph. Have the class formulate a question that would be answered if it read the text.

- Model: "We are going to read this text on dogs together. As we read, think about what the author is telling you about dogs. Read the text aloud. What is something you learned about dogs? Yes, some dogs come in many different sizes. Let's turn that into a question. What do dogs look like?" Write the question and answer on chart paper. Do more examples until you have assessed all students.
- As a lesson extension, give students a list of facts and have them formulate questions about a text that has been read. The mature learners can get started right away; the typical learners should meet in a small group with the teacher right away to start together; and the emerging learners can illustrate what they have learned until it is time to meet with the teacher to complete the task together.
- As always, conclude with a quick group meeting for students to talk about what they have learned.

A RAN chart or KWL chart is an effective strategy to use with explanatory text as it is with descriptive texts. You may also create your own graphic organizer as we have done below.

The following lesson is based in the book *Now You Know Question and Answer Book*, published by Wishing Well books.

This book contains wonderful text access features for young children. It has a table of contents, simple diagrams, and headings.

1. Share the front and back covers of the book with the students. Tell the students that this book has answers to many questions young children have about nature, animals, how things work, and more.
2. Share the table of contents with the students. Have students predict/guess what they might learn in the book based on the front/back cover, illustrations, and table of contents.
3. Have students generate their own questions that may be answered in this book. Record these questions on a graphic organizer. Make sure you display this chart so that it may be referred to throughout the lesson.

Questions We Have	Questions Answered	Research Needed

4. Choose one of each text access feature, simple diagram, and heading to explain to the students. Have students share how these features help them to better understand the information.
5. Refer back to the chart. Use the features in the book to investigate the answers to the students' questions—table of contents, headings, diagrams.

After reading, create your own class question-and-answer book. Choose a topic that is aligned with what you are currently studying in other content areas. Remember that the format of an explanatory text includes questions as headings within the book. Have students generate questions about the topic. (You may even refer to "before reading" questions that were generated on a KWL or RAN chart that was completed before a topic was studied.) Students may generate new questions or generate questions based on what they have learned about the topic to create the class book.

Once students have decided on the questions that will be used in the book, research the answers to the questions by using a variety of resources, such as Internet sites, other nonfiction books, reference books, videos, and magazines. This will provide a perfect opportunity to introduce young students to research and several types of informational resources. As you research, create access features to include in the book, such as a chart, diagram, or illustration. Have students create labels for these features. You may even find photographs to include, for which students can write captions.

When creating a book like this with young students, it is best to work on the book a little at a time over the course of a week. Do only two main questions for younger students so that you have time to do some research and add access features to the book. Here is a breakdown of the process.

Day 1: Choose a Topic

- Brainstorm topics students are studying.
- Brainstorm topics students know about.
- Brainstorm topics students want to learn about.
- Choose one topic in which students have some background knowledge but can also learn more from further research.

Day 2: Generate Questions

- Generate two main questions about the topic.
- Be sure that the questions will enable you to create access features such as charts, diagrams, photographs, or illustrations.
- Choose questions that students have some background information on but require further research.

Day 3: Answer/Research Question 1

- Record information that students already know that will answer the question. Be sure to record information neatly onto sentence strips or strips of paper so that it can be pasted onto the final book.
- Research using other nonfiction books, Internet sites, videos, resource books, and so on, to provide in-depth answers to the question. Remember, you do not need to read nonfiction books in full. You may refer to the index or table of contents to read only the parts of the book that refer to your question.
- Create an access feature that is aligned with the information found. You may also find photographs to include, and have students create labels for the photographs.

Day 4: Answer/Research Question 2

- Record information that students already know that will answer the question. Be sure to record information neatly onto sentence strips or strips of paper so that it can be pasted onto the final book.

- Research using other nonfiction books, Internet sites, videos, resource books, and so on, to provide in-depth answers to the question. Remember, you do not need to read nonfiction books in full. You may refer to the index or table of contents to read only the parts of the book that refer to your question.
- Create an access feature that is aligned with the information found. You may also find photographs to include, and have students create labels for the photographs.

Day 5: Pull It All Together

- Use large construction paper so there is plenty of room to paste your written information and access features. Extra space may be used for students to create illustrations, labels, or captions to the page.
- You will need five pieces of construction paper. Use one page for the cover, one for the table of contents, one for each question, and one for references.
- Create a table of contents based on your questions.
- Write each question heading on a separate page.
- Paste the written information that was compiled to answer each question under each heading.
- Paste the access features that were created on the proper pages.
- Add any additional illustrations, photographs, labels, and so on.
- Illustrate the cover (this may be done as a center activity at another time).
- Write the references used to answer the questions onto the last page.
- Bind the book together.

MORE COMPLEX TEXT STRUCTURES

You will be teaching more complex text structures with explicit whole classroom activities. Oral discussion and read-alouds are two very effective basic strategies for introducing these concepts. Modeling more complex structures, such as comparison, response, causation, or persuasive through read-alouds within the classroom, helps our youngest readers develop strategies for understanding all types of nonfiction.

A comparison text explains the similarities and differences in two or more objects or ideas. Young students may experience this type of text when they are learning about topics in science. An example is the difference between an insect and a spider or a reptile and an amphibian. Students are also exposed to comparisons when they talk about the similarities and differences between ideas and fictional stories, such as versions of a fairy tale.

Other comparisons may include a book that tells about how different animals care for their babies or how different cultures dress. Giving students the opportunity to experience comparisons outside of a text will help them comprehend the material when they experience comparisons within a text.

A response text presents a problem for the reader to solve. Although this structure may seem complex for young readers, there are many that can be used as effective read-alouds. Response texts help spark rich discussion even in the youngest grades. This structure is most useful in kindergarten and first-grade classrooms when studying Earth Day and recycling. Students can have many discussions on what they can do to protect our Earth and environment.

A causation, or cause-and-effect, text presents how one thing can affect another. This type of text can be too complex for young students to read themselves; however, these texts can be used in K–1 classrooms. As with response texts, cause/effect texts can be used when studying Earth Day and ways to protect our environment. This type of text also sparks rich discussion because students can come up with ways they can affect our environment in a positive way.

A persuasive text convinces a reader to take a stance on an issue. This type of text may appear as a read-aloud or an article in a children's newsletter or magazine in the younger grades. Elections during the month of November provide natural opportunities to explore this structure through class discussions that focus around elections and what they are. Many schools also have student councils that also include the younger grades. These student councils often discuss school issues and may read and create persuasive texts.

Model within instructional activities: For young readers, the following structures are modeled through read alouds and instructional activities.

Comparison

This type of text compares two or more concepts, ideas, or topics. Comparison circles serve as an effective graphic organizer to use if only two concepts are compared. Label each circle before reading. As you read the text aloud, write words or phrases into the comparison circles. Discuss the likenesses and differences of the concepts as you read by referring to the comparison circles. Be sure to link information from the text to prior learning. If more than two concepts are compared, as in the text "Everybody Cooks Rice," have students choose two or three to compare. You can create separate comparison circle charts on different days to compare different cultures in the book.

Comparison Text that explains relationships between two or more things	To note likeness and differences between two or more objects or ideas	Varies and is used in content area texts. Keywords: like, unlike, resemble, different from, same as, alike, similar	Students complete compare/contrast organizer
Response Texts about a social, political or environmental dilemma	To present a problem for the reader to provide a solution	Varies and is used in math, science, and social studies Keywords: the problem is, the question is, one reason for the problem, a solution, one answer is	Students brainstorm ways to solve or prevent the problem
Causation; *cause-effect* Texts about how one thing affects another	Ideas presented in a causal relationship that is either stated or implied.	Varies and is used in content area textbooks, articles Keywords: therefore, consequently, because, as a result of, since, the reasons for	Students can write about ways their actions affect others

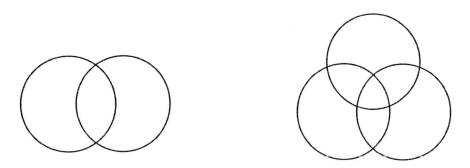

The following lesson is based on the book *Everybody Cooks Rice*, by Norah Dooley. This book is written in narrative form. In this form, the author compares how different cultures prepare the same food differently—namely, rice. Students have the opportunity to see the likenesses and differences in cultures from around the world by interacting with this text. This text also provides recipes for the rice dishes that each culture shares in this book. This lesson will be formatted as a read-aloud.

- Before reading this text, ask students about the different cultures we have in the classroom. What special foods do they eat? What countries are their families from?
- Share the illustrations in the book. Ask students what they notice about the people in the story. Do they all appear to be from the same part of the world? What details in the picture show the students that this book has many different cultures in it?

Response

A text elicits a response from the reader. Response texts are effective when studying Earth Day. Students in the younger grades tend to do a lot of activities that tie into saving the environment: reduce, reuse, recycle. They also learn about different kinds of habitats and how we can protect the animals that live there. A favorite book to use as a model response text is *The Empty Lot*, by Dale Fife, illustrated by Jim Arnosky. This book is about a man who had an empty wooded lot for sale. After several visits to the lot, he noticed that the lot is being used and occupied by several different creatures. He imagined what would happen to these creatures if a bulldozer turned the lot into a parking lot. He then marked his empty lot as "occupied" and crossed out the "For Sale" sign.

The author presents this story in a way that allows for young students to be able to respond. Make sure you let the students know that the author wrote this story to help readers think about how they feel about what happened and that they will have the opportunity to share their opinions during and after reading.

While reading this story to the students, reinforce the key vocabulary that was introduced prior to the lesson. Refer to the picture cards that were used during the "before reading" lesson. Before reading, students discussed how they thought losing the empty lot would affect each animal on the picture cards. During reading, more information is given. Have students elaborate further on what each animal is and how its life would be different if the lot was changed. Model your connections as you read: "I used to collect red salamanders like the one in the story. I would find them under rocks or in the wet leaves. I think the salamander in the story would not be able to survive if all the rocks and leaves were taken away."

You can elaborate on your connection by linking your thinking to what had been previously taught about salamanders. "Remember what we had learned about salamanders in science. They are amphibians, and they need to live in moist places." Invite students to share connections as you read. Encourage them to also link their thinking to information that had been previously learned.

Point out the text features in the font—italics for the animal sounds, bold print for the signs. "What do you notice about the print in the text? I see that the animal sounds are in italics. The author wants us to notice that the animals are happy in the empty lot." As you read the rest of the story, continue to reinforce key vocabulary and stop to make connections and share thoughts.

Again, the following lesson is based on the book *The Empty Lot*, by Dale Fife. This book is in narrative form. The author chose to write a narrative to convey his message. Even though this is not a nonfiction book, it clearly presents a problem for the reader to solve—a problem that exists in the real world. This book is a wonderful resource to share on Earth Day. To present this structure, the lesson will be formatted as a read-aloud.

1. Share the title and author of the story.
2. Share the pictures from the front and back covers and title page.
3. Have students share predictions about the story.
4. Introduce key vocabulary. Students may not be familiar with the following words: *lot, acres, woods, meadow, abandoned, occupied.*
5. Word/picture sort: Choose animals/critters from the book to use as a picture/word-sorting activity. Be sure to label each picture and read the labels with the students. Have students sort the animals into categories. After all pictures are sorted, have the students name each category. Here are some examples from the story: *chickadee, woodpecker, sparrow, blue jay, frog, cricket, ants, beetles, snail, worm, squirrel, dragonfly.*
6. Read the story aloud to the students. Talk about how the animals from the picture sort may be affected if all the trees and plants from the empty lot were destroyed.

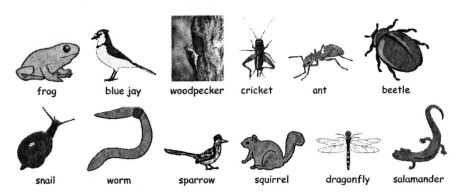

frog   blue jay   woodpecker   cricket   ant   beetle

snail   worm   sparrow   squirrel   dragonfly   salamander

Persuasive

The following lesson is based on the book *Once There Was Tree*, by Natalia Romanova. This book is written in narrative form but does imply the question "Who does the tree stump belong to?" While reading this book, the reader may take a stance on the ownership of the tree stump. This book does contain labels as text access features. To present this structure, this lesson will be presented as a read-aloud.

- Show the front and back cover. Ask students what they think this book may be about.
- Introduce key vocabulary: *bark beetle, woodsman, ants, titmouse, frog, earwig, tree stump.* These terms will be further defined through the labels in the text. Place a picture of each of these terms in a pocket chart.

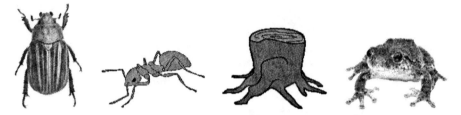

- Do a "picture walk." Have students use details in the pictures to explain what is happening in the story. Note the text access feature labels on the pictures. Have students take pictures out of the pocket chart to match with the items being labeled in the text.

While reading a persuasive text, model your opinion about what is being said in the text. Encourage students to also share their opinions. Link opinions to what has previously been learned in class. Be sure to reinforce key vocabulary while reading so that students can see the words being used in context. For example, picture cards were created to introduce key vocabulary words for the story *Once There Was a Tree*, by Natalia Romanova. As you read, refer to these picture cards and see if students can match the picture cards to the text as you are reading.

Remember, this book is a persuasive text. Model your thoughts about the context of the story as you read the book aloud to the students. "The author wants us to think about who this tree stump belongs to. As I read the story, I am noticing that the tree stump belongs to lots of things. I learned that beetles lay their eggs on it, and the bear likes to sharpen its claws on the stump. I think that the stump belongs to lots of things. Who do you think the tree belongs to?"

Writing activities for persuasive texts may include creating a piece of writing that displays their stance on a topic. Each student may create a poster to advertise his or her point of view or convince the audience of something. An example can be creating "Endangered Animals" posters displaying facts about a specific animal and why it should be saved. Another example is to create an Earth Day mural:

- Cut out a large circle out of blue poster paper (symbolizing Earth).
- Cut out land forms using green paper.
- Provide each student with a land form.
- Have each student write ways to protect the environment on each of the land forms.
- Paste the land forms onto the blue circle.
- Display your "Earth" where students can react to it.

Causation

The causation structure is not common in nonfiction in the early grades. Causation may be found within other text structures. For example, if you turn on a switch, a light will go on. If you leave ice cream in the sun, it will melt. When encountering causation, talk about cause and effect. "What caused . . . to happen?" "What was the effect of . . . " "If we did . . . instead, what would the effect have been?"

Create a cause/effect chart with the students to help them further understand the concepts. Fill out the chart with the students as they read through the text. You may talk about causation while learning about a topic or several topics as a review. This chart may also be used to review or reinforce learning as an "after reading" activity. Books about the effects of weather or pollution are appropriate for the younger grades because students are able to connect to the concepts.

Cause / Why It Happened	Effect / What Happened

EIGHT
PUTTING IT ALL TOGETHER

Teaching nonfiction is an important aspect of the primary grade curriculum. Students will be exposed to nonfiction throughout their lives, and they need to know how to tackle the information being presented to them. Nonfiction occurs in many forms—posters, magazines, textbooks, menus, schedules, recipes, directions, newspapers, articles, web pages, and so on. Exposure to these types of texts throughout life exceeds that of narrative fiction.

While teaching characteristics of fiction is important, it is critical that students are explicitly taught all of the features and structures that occur in nonfiction so they can maximize learning as they read all types of text. Curriculums need to have a balance so that students can comprehend all types of genres as they strive to become independent readers.

When teaching nonfiction, as with any other skill being taught, the teacher needs to begin with a piece of the topic and then expand, building connections along the way.

Planning is key. When using this book, begin with "before reading" strategies and choose tasks that are comfortable for you. Begin with the text access features and student activities you are familiar with. At the same time, plan the "during" and "after" activities in the same manner. Modeling a think-aloud is the best way to accomplish this. After reading, have students apply the skill in writing. Create an assignment that links with the text structure and allows students to refer to text access features from the piece studied.

Lesson plan templates are included in this chapter. Some of these templates are more explicit than others. We included different types of templates to accommodate varied teaching styles. Whichever template you choose, be sure to include "before," "during," and "after" reading activities to maximize student understanding.

The first template is a planning guide. It sorts lesson components into a before/during/after format and gives an explanation of how each aspect should be formatted. This template is also available in a blank version so that it may be used as a lesson planner. The second template is an organizer to help teachers script lesson objectives, activities, and materials for each part of the lesson. This organizer serves as a planner. The final organizer follows a lesson format and focuses on what the teacher and student will do during the literacy block. It may be used in conjunction with any of the other templates. You may also use these templates as a resource to create your own.

ASSESSMENT

Ongoing instruction is based on continual assessment, either formally or informally. As a teacher, you are continually assessing what students know and understand through questioning and observation. When you want to conclude a topic of study, it is important to assess the cumulative student learning. In the early grades, assessment of learning can take many forms, from a paper-and-pencil test to looking at student work to games. When it is time to assess students for learning, a game format is helpful for this age group.

Riddles

Teacher prep. The teacher should write three clues that get increasingly more obvious about the answer, as well as a list of the answer words that the students can have in front of them. The riddles should be cut into individual strips and put in a bag.
   Materials.

1. Bingo chips or markers
2. An answer sheet
3. Bag of riddles

Implementation. In a small group setting, the teacher hands each child an answer sheet and one marker. Each student can take a turn and pull a riddle out of the bag. The teacher reads the riddle, and as the students figure it out, they can put the bingo/marker chip on the answer. The teacher can observe when students figure out the answer and if they are correct.
   "Today we are going to play a game. I am giving you a sheet with words about our study of bees and one bingo chip. Each of you will have a turn to choose a riddle from the bag like this [*teacher demonstrates taking a paper out of the bag*] and give it to me to read. As I read each clue, try to figure out what I am talking about. When you think you know the

answer, put your bingo chip on your sheet on the correct space. Put your chip on as soon as you know, even if I haven't finished the clues. You can change your mind as I read more clues. Let's try one together."
Differentiate.

1. Students create riddles themselves and answer each others.
2. Students can illustrate the answers.

Bingo

Teacher prep. The teacher should create topic specific bingo cards from the model in this book or from one of the many Internet sites found through a search engine. The cards can be any combination of words and pictures depending on the level of your students. Be sure to have a caller card (answer) for each different space on the bingo boards. The students can match exactly to the square, or the caller cards can be "clues" to the squares on the bingo board.
Materials.

1. Bingo chips or markers
2. Bingo cards
3. Caller cards for the bingo game

Implementation. In a small or whole group setting, the teacher hands each child a board and some markers. The teacher or a student can choose a caller/answer card and read it to the group. The students place a marker on the appropriate square. When a student has a completed row he or she should yell "BINGO!" Have the student check all answers for another review.

"Today we are going to play a game. I am giving you a bingo sheet with words about our study of bees and bingo chips. I will read a definition of the word; after I read each definition, try to figure out what I am talking about. When you think you know the answer, put your bingo chip on your sheet on the correct space. When you have four chips in a row, yell "BINGO!" We will check the answers together. Let's try one now as a group. The first definition is "A bee's home is called a . . . " The answer is "hive." Please place a bingo chip on the word "hive" if you have it on your card. Now I will read the definitions until someone has bingo." The teacher continues until someone has bingo. "Ok, Matilda has bingo. Matilda, read the words you covered one at a time, and we will check to be sure the definition has been read." The teacher checks the definitions as the words are read and gets confirmation from the students.

Turn and Talk

Teacher prep. The teacher should assign weekly turn-and-talk partners, and model how to do turn-and-talk with the class before it is needed.

Materials. None.

Implementation. The teacher instructs the students to turn and tell their partner three (four, five, six, . . .) things they learned during the lesson, unit, and so on. The teacher then calls on several groups to share with the class. Have them use phrases such as "My partner learned . . . "

"Now we are going to turn and talk to our partner. Remember to stay on topic. What is the topic? Great Sam, that is correct. We are going to turn and tell our partner three things we learned about bees. When the timer goes off, we will share. You may begin." Teacher starts the minute timer. When the timer goes off, call on three groups to share with the whole class. Model the consistent language, such as "My partner learned . . . " "Sam, tell me what your partner learned."

Class Book

Teacher prep. The teacher prepares book pages with subtitles or sentence starters depending on the age group. Students can complete one or two book pages depending on the number of students and amount of infor-mation. Some examples of sentence starters are "The bees live in hives and the drones protect the queen. You can find bees in every country. There are 20 types of bees. The colors of bees are . . ."

Materials.

1. Prepared pages
2. Writing and illustrating instruments
3. Word banks or reference books

Implementation. The teacher models the completion of a page.

"Today we are going to create pages for a class book with all of the information we learned about bees. Each of the pages has a sentence starter (subtitle) for you to complete with information you remember from our study. Here is a page with 'You can find . . . in . . . ' I will fill it in like this: 'You can find bees in every country.' Now I want to give more information to the reader. I can add more facts, like what kind of home they live in. What kind of home do they live in? Correct, they live in hives. I'll write that next. 'Bees live in hives.' Now to give the reader more information, I will draw a picture. Hmmm, what are some ways I can illustrate this? Yes, I can draw a hive with a back-ground of trees, or I can draw a picture of Earth with a bee and hive on it or just countries with hives. Very good. Now you will get a page to complete. When we are all done, the pages will be put into a book for the class library."

Differentiate. The teacher passes out pages and can differentiate by the content of the page given to each particular student.

Questions and Answers

Teacher prep. This is like the popular game show *Jeopardy*, where the students are provided the answer and have to formulate a question. Prepare facts about bees from the previous lessons. Each fact should be on a separate piece of paper.

Materials.

1. Paper with facts
2. Pencils
3. Resource books

Implementation. In a small group, the teacher models *who, what, when, why, where,* and *how* questions. The students create questions from answers about the topic and then share. These can also become a center activity.

"Today we will write *who, what, when, why, where,* and *how* questions about bees. First pick a fact sheet; this will be your answer. Here's one:

Lesson Aspect	Application	Materials Needed
What will the student learn?	Photographs help me figure out what the author is trying to tell me.	Model text
What background is needed?	What is a photograph?	Various resources that contain photographs: books, web pages, articles, etc.
	How to fill in a graphic organizer	
		Completed graphic organizers
What will the teacher model?	Think aloud as teacher shares model text	Model text
What will students do during reading/modeling?	Complete a graphic organizer highlighting details in the photographs	Describe it!
What will students do independently or in groups?	Write a paragraph describing a photograph in the text.	Text at independent or instructional level; notebook or paper
What is the Curriculum Connection?	B1. Identify or infer the author's use of structure/organizational patterns	CT State LA Frameworks—aligned with NAEP Standards

Lesson Aspect	Application	Materials Needed
What will the student learn?		
What background is needed?		
What will the teacher model?		
What will students do during reading/modeling?		
What will students do independently or in groups?		
What is the Curriculum Connection?		

'Bees live in hives.' This can be a *where* question: 'Where do bees live?' The next fact sheet states that bees make honey. This can be a *what* question: 'What do bees do?' Now it is your turn. Take a sheet, read the fact, and then think of a question. You can ask the question to me or a neighbor before you write it to be sure it makes sense."

WHOLE CLASS/SMALL GROUP PLANNING IDEAS

Shared reading
RAN chart
Modified KWL chart
Anticipation guide
Small group

1. RAN chart (use manila folders to make portable RAN charts)
   a. Includes background knowledge, new facts learned, questions raised.
   b. Students confirm or revise background knowledge while reading.
2. Main idea
   a. Have students use sticky notes to write the main for each section of text.

3. Details
   a. Have students use sticky notes to write details that support the main idea for each section of text.
4. Text features
   a. Have students tell how text access features, such as charts, diagrams, and captions, helped them understand the information.
   b. Students may create their own access feature to show information that was learned.
5. Writing
   a. Have students write about what they learned using a main idea/ detail format. Students should include headings and at least one access feature in their writing.
6. Make a connection.
   a. Have students write about a connection they have to the information learned.
7. Find an article that relates to the topic.
   a. Have students add new information to the RAN chart.
   b. Have students highlight facts in the article.
   c. Have students complete comparison circles to compare/contrast information from the book and the article.

Nonfiction Planning Template

Book Title: _____

Content Area: _____

Topic: _____

Before Reading
Background knowledge/prior teaching connection:
_____

Vocabulary:

Text access feature:

Comprehension skill:

During Reading
Purpose:

Group 1:

Group 2:

Group 3:
_____

After Reading
Questions that focus on content (enable students to use access features):

Writing assignment to demonstrate learning:

Before Reading *Graphic organizer /* *text access feature / think-aloud*	During Reading	After Reading

Preview
  ■ Content
  ■ Vocabulary
  ■ Organization
 	
Predict
 	
Connect to background knowledge
 	
Vocabulary
  ■ Glossary
  ■ Context clues
  ■ Structural analysis
  ■ Word origins
 	
Comprehension skill
 	
Text access feature(s) focus
 	
Think-aloud
	Set purpose
	  ■ Focus on text access features
	
	Small groups
	  ■ Some read independently
	    o Record questions
	    o Record difficult words
	  ■ Some read with support
	    o Read in sections
	    o Pause for questions
	    o Monitor comprehension
	  ■ Reciprocal reading roles
	    o Questioning, predicting, summarizing
	    o Students ask questions that can be answered by using the text
	    o Students seek information to confirm/revise predictions
		Build comprehension
		  ■ Connect prior thoughts to reading
		    o Analyze text
		Apply the skill
		  ■ Organize thinking
		
		Demonstrate learning: writing
		  ■ Write in the same genre
		  ■ Apply vocabulary to writing
		
		Access the learning
		  ■ Ask questions that focus on content
		  ■ Ask questions that enable students to use text access features
		  ■ Ask students to explain graphs, maps, charts, etc.

Linking Reading and Content Learning		
Read leveled books before the content area is introduced to give background knowledge.		
Make connections between evidence and explanations.		

Before Reading *Graphic organizer /* *text access feature / think-aloud*	During Reading	After Reading

Preview
  • Content
  • Vocabulary
  • Organization
 	
Predict
 	
Connect to background knowledge
 	
Vocabulary:
 	
Comprehension skill:
 	
Text access feature(s) focus:
 	
Think-aloud
	Set purpose
	
	Small groups
	  •
	
	  •
		Build comprehension
		
		Apply the skill
		
		Demonstrate learning:
		writing
		  •
		
		  •
		
		Access the learning
		  •
		
		  •

Linking Reading and Content Learning		

Materials to build/activate background knowledge:

Teaching/learning connection:

Appendix of Blacklines:
Graphic Organizers, Templates

Text Cues and Graphic Organizers

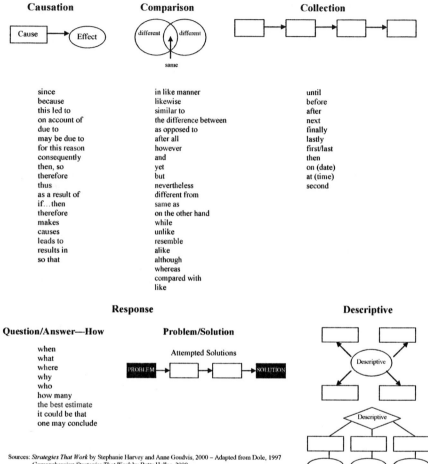

Causation

since
because
this led to
on account of
due to
may be due to
for this reason
consequently
then, so
therefore
thus
as a result of
if…then
therefore
makes
causes
leads to
results in
so that

Comparison

in like manner
likewise
similar to
the difference between
as opposed to
after all
however
and
yet
but
nevertheless
different from
same as
on the other hand
while
unlike
resemble
alike
although
whereas
compared with
like

Collection

until
before
after
next
finally
lastly
first/last
then
on (date)
at (time)
second

Response

Question/Answer—How

when
what
where
why
who
how many
the best estimate
it could be that
one may conclude

Problem/Solution

Descriptive

Sources: *Strategies That Work* by Stephanie Harvey and Anne Goudvis, 2000 – Adapted from Dole, 1997
Comprehension Strategies That Work by Betty Hollas, 2000

Anticipation Guide

Title: _____

Statement	True	False	Unsure

What We Think We Know	Yes, We Were Right	New Facts	Wonderings

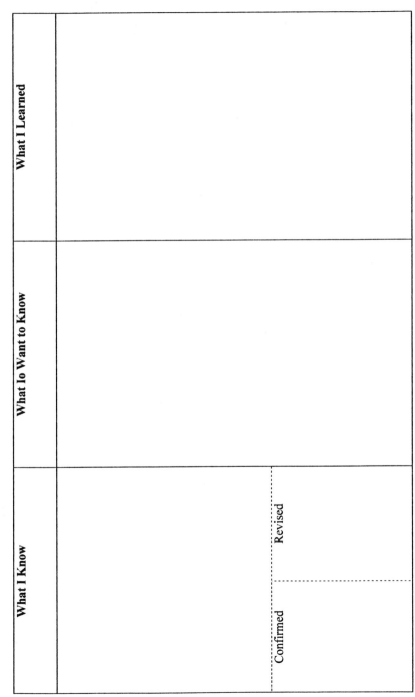

Modified KWL Chart

What I Know	What Io Want to Know	What I Learned

Confirmed

Revised

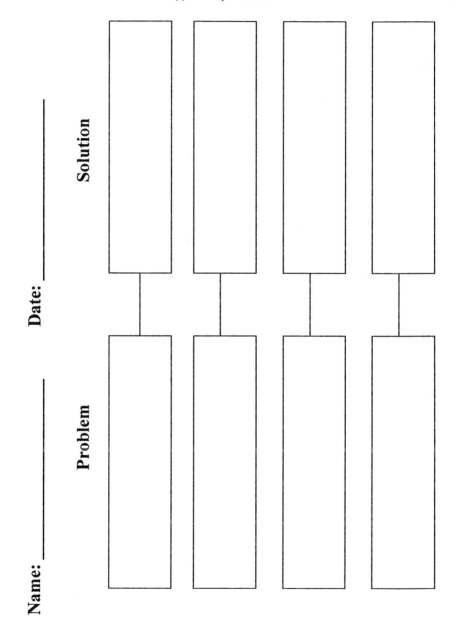

Name: _____ Date: _____

Problem   Solution

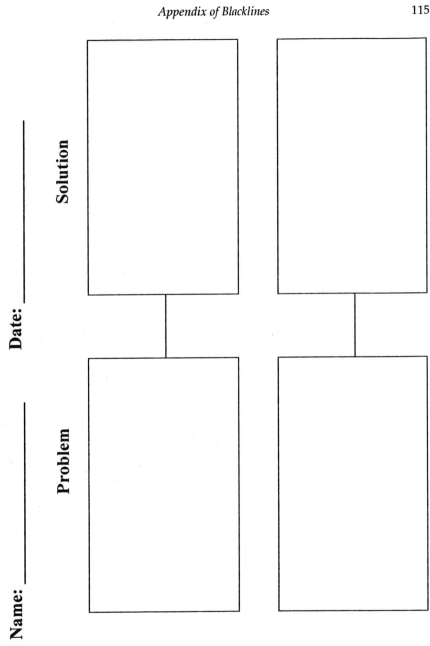

Name: _____

Date: _____

Problem

Solution

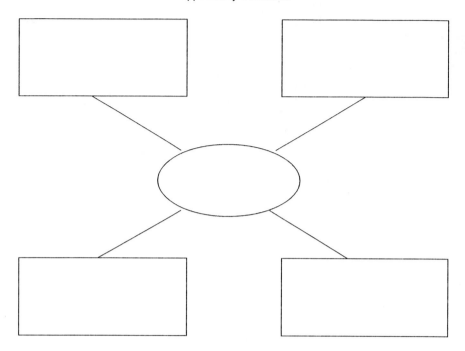

Name: _____ **Date:** _____

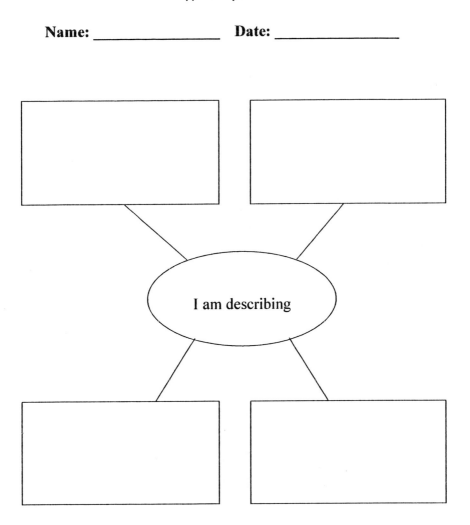

Book title: _____

Name: _____

Focus Features: _____

Feature	Page Number	Describe it!	How does this help?

Describe It!

Name: _____   **Topic:** _____

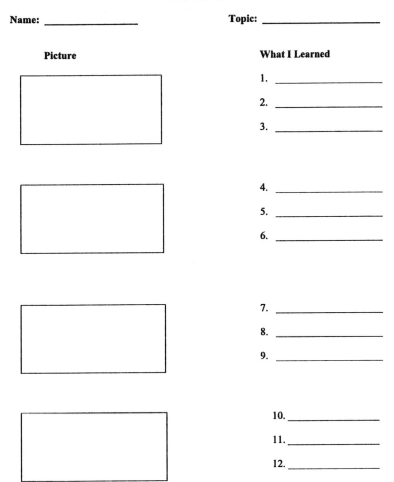

Picture

What I Learned

1. _____
2. _____
3. _____

4. _____
5. _____
6. _____

7. _____
8. _____
9. _____

10. _____
11. _____
12. _____

Appendix of Blacklines

3-2-1- Chart

3 THINGS I LEARNED	2 THINGS I CONNECTED WITH	1 QUESTION I STILL HAVE
•	•	•
•	•	
•		

Name: _____

Date: _____

Cause

Effect

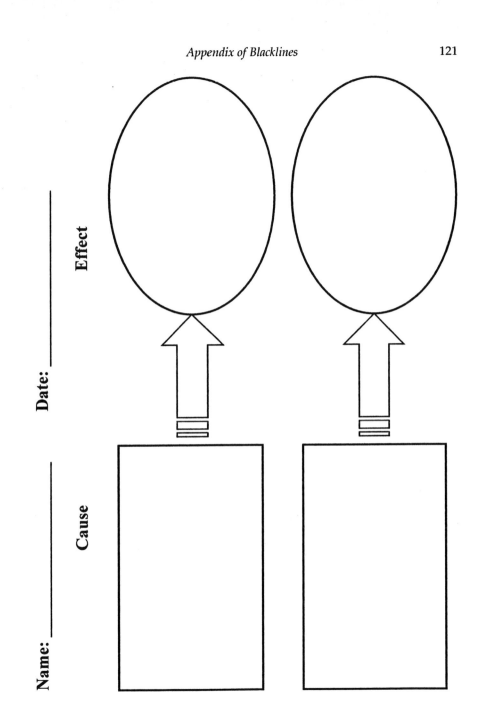

Appendix of Blacklines

Name: _____ **Date:** _____

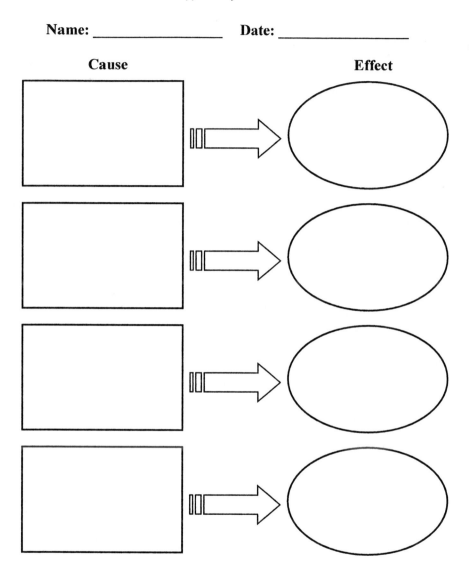

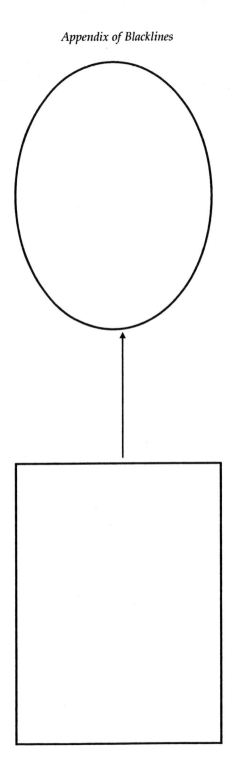

Name: _____

Cause/Why it happened	Effect/What happened

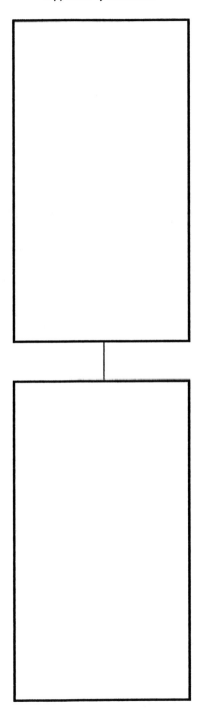

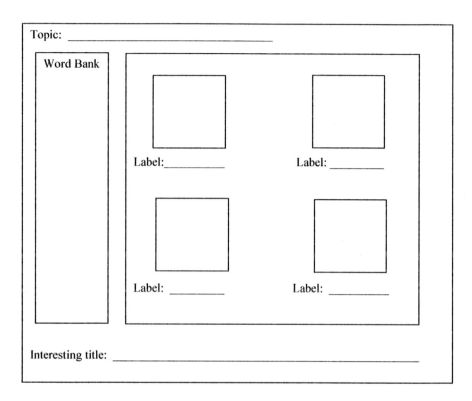

Word Web

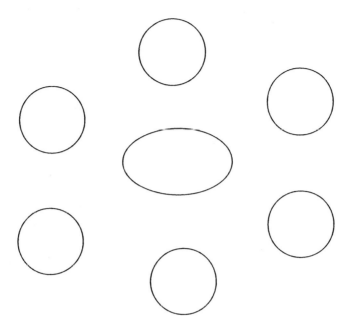

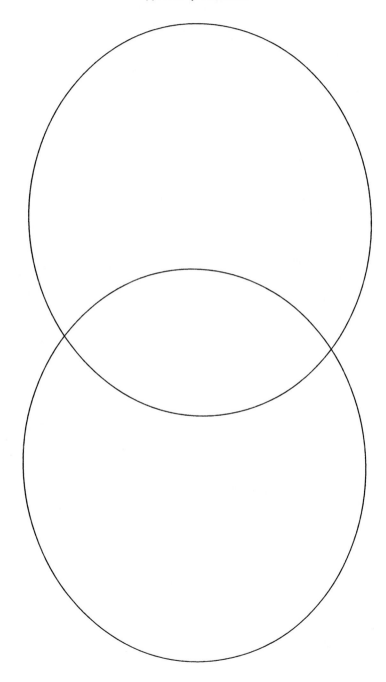

Name: _____

Date: _____

I am comparing

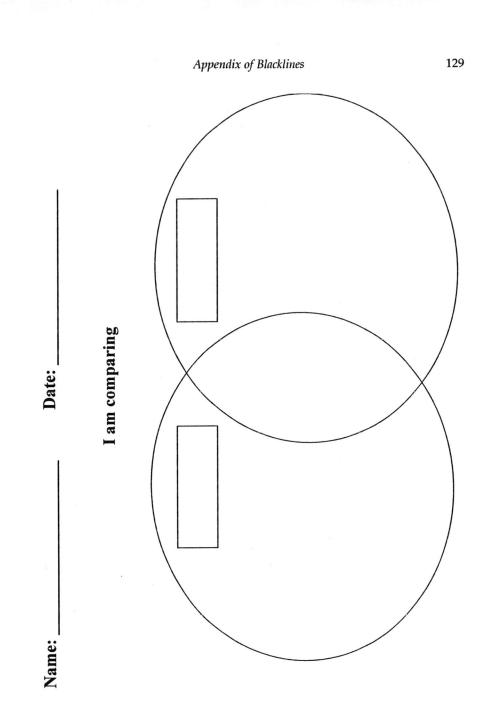

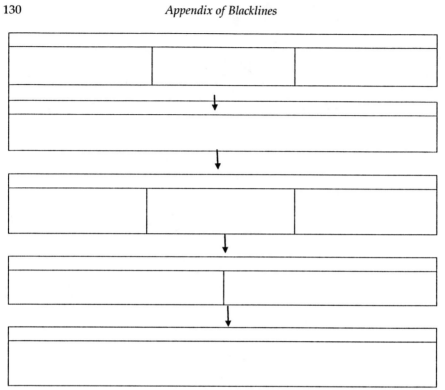

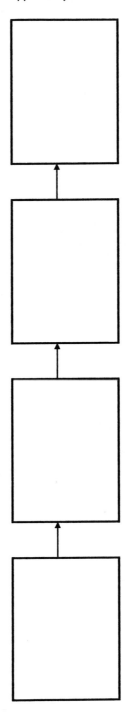

Name: _____ Date: _____

Sequence chain for

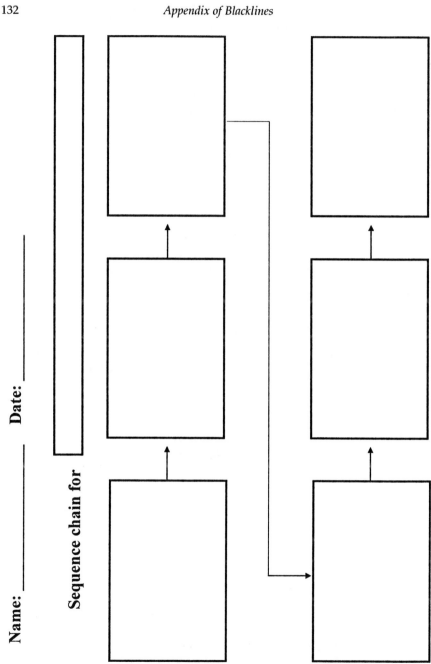

ANNOTATED BIBLIOGRAPHY

Boyles, N. 2004. *Constructing Meaning through Kid-Friendly Strategies Instruction.* Gainesville, FL: Maupin House, Inc.

Carlisle, J., and M. Rice. 2002. *Improving Reading Comprehension: Researched Based Principles and Practices.* Baltimore, MD: York Press, Inc.

Marzano, R. 2004. *Classroom Strategies That Work.* Upper Saddle River, NJ: Prentice Hall.

Mowery, S. 1995. *Reading and Writing Comprehension Strategies.* Harrisburg, PA: Instructional Support Team Publications.

Oczkus, L. 2003. *Reciprocal Teaching Strategies at Work: Improving Reading Comprehension, Grades 2–6.* Newark, DE: International Reading Association.

Stead, T. 2006. *Reality Checks.* Portland, ME: Stenhouse.

STRUCTURE: DESCRIPTIVE

Animals Day and Night, by Katherine Kenah. 2004. School Specialty Publishing, OH. This level 1 reader text uses headings and clear photographs to describe animals that are active in the day or night.

A Day with the Baker, by Kathleen Collins. 2004. Rosen Publishing Group, NY. This book describes what a baker does on a typical day. The math skill of telling time by the quarter hour is also reinforced in this book. Text access features include photographs, captions, clock diagrams, table of contents, glossary, and index. This book may also be used as a procedural text.

Diving Dolphins, by Karen Wallace. 2001. DK Publishing, NY. This level 1 reader book contains photographs, labels, insets, and a picture word list/glossary.

DK Eye Wonder Series: *Weather,* by Laurie Mack; *Whales and Dolphins,* by Caroline Bingham; *Space,* by Simon Holland. 2004. Dorling Kindersley, NY. Books in this series contain text features: table of contents, index, glossary, sidebars, photographs, captions, maps, diagrams, and fun facts.

Earth Matters: An Encyclopedia of Ecology, by DK Publishing. 2008. DK Publishing, NY. This book contains a wealth of information on our Earth, the environment, and animal habitats around the world. All text features are included—insets, sidebars, diagrams, photographs, captions, timelines, table of contents, glossary, and index.

How Everything Was Invented, by the Brainwaves. 2006. DK Publishing, NY. Facts are presented through pictures, captions, and diagrams. Text features include table of contents, pictures with captions, foldouts, index, glossary, diagrams, timelines, headings, and subheadings.

Poster Book Series: *Under the Sea, Petting Farm, Horses and Friends, Dream Horses*, and *Horse Breeds*, by Andy Case, Mark Faulkner, and Edward Sertel. 2005. Storey Publishing, MA. These books contain detailed photographs with clear descriptions for each photo. Text features include photographs, headings, and subheadings.

Rockets and Spaceships, by Karen Wallace. 2001. DK Publishing, NY. This level 1 reader uses clear photographs and insets to highlight details and includes a picture glossary to describe spaceships and space equipment that is used today.

Science Kids: Rocks and Fossils, by Chris Pellant. 2007. Kingfisher, MA. Text features include headings, subheadings, index, sidebars, photographs, captions, and words with definitions. Experiments in a procedural format are provided at the end of the text.

Science Kid Series: *Oceans and Seas*, by Nicola Davies. 2004. Kingfisher, MA. Each topic is clearly described under each heading and subheading. Text access features include headings, subheadings, diagrams, insets, photographs, table of contents, index, words with definitions. This book also contains a how-to/procedural section with many projects related to the topics in this book.

See Inside Science, by Alex Frith and Colin King. 2007. Usborne Publishing, US. Each topic is described through captions and tabs that open to reveal more pictures and facts. Text features include pictures, captions, words and definitions, diagrams, flip-up facts, and a table of contents.

Sharks! by Anne Schreiber. 2008. National Geographic Publishers, Washington, DC. Diagrams, labels, captions, photographs, headings, sidebars, insets, and labels teach the reader about sharks.

Strange Animals, by Robyn O'Sullivan. 2004. National Geographic, Washington, DC. This book describes many unusual animals. Text access features include photographs and captions, table of contents, and glossary.

Tale of a Tadpole, by Karen Wallace. 1998. DK Publishing, NY. This level 1 reader book uses photographs, labels, insets, and a picture word list/glossary to describe how a frog egg becomes a tadpole and then a frog.

Time for Kids, Bears! by Time for Kids. 2005. Time, Inc., NY. This level 1 reader book describes the life of a bear and adds facts using sidebar and photographs.

A Trip to the Dentist, by Penny Smith. 2006. DK Publishing, NY. Photographs, insets, and drawings teach the reader about going to the dentist.

Volcanoes! by Anne Schreiber. 2008. National Geographic Publishers, Washington, DC. Diagrams, labels, sidebars, photographs, insets, maps, captions, a table of contents, and headings are used to convey the information along with the text.

Voyages Series: *Rainforest*, by Jenny Johnson, forward and questions by Dr. Nalini Nadkarni. 2006. Kingfisher, MA. This book contains information on life in the rainforest. Text features include photographs, captions, words with definitions, headings subheadings, overlays, sidebars, and a glossary.

Weather and Climate, by Rebecca L. Johnson. 2003. National Geographic, Washington, DC. This book explains the many aspects of weather and climate. Text access features include photographs and captions, diagrams and maps, sidebars, chapter titles and subheadings, table of contents, glossary, and index.

Whatever the Weather, by Karen Wallace. 1999. DK Publishing, NY. Weather for four seasons is described in this level 1 reader book through the use of photographs, labels, insets, and a picture word list/glossary.

Wild Baby Animals, by Karen Wallace. 2000. DK Publishing, NY. This level 1 reader book contains photographs, labels, insets, and a picture word list/glossary.

STRUCTURE: RECOUNT

Barack Obama: An American Story, by Roberta Edwards. 2008. Penguin Group, NY. This biography contains the text features photographs, captions, and maps.

A Day in the Life of a Police Officer, by Linda Howard. 2001. DK Publishing, NY. Inserts and photographs take the reader through a day of a police officer and the equipment he uses.

First Day at Gymnastics, by Anita Ganeri. 2002. DK Publishing, NY. This day in the life of a gymnast uses a simple sentence structure and includes labels and a picture dictionary.

Free at Last: The Story of Martin Luther King Jr., by Angela Bull. 2000. DK Publishing, NY. The bibliography contains the text features table of contents, glossary, index, photographs, diagrams, and sidebars.

I Want to Be a Ballerina, by Annabel Blackledge. 2005. DK Publishing, NY. Photographs, labels, and insets help the reader learn about a first ballet lesson.

Presidents of the United States, by Time for Kids. 2006. HarperCollins, NY. This biographical book contains the text features photographs, cutaways, labels, captions, timelines, index, table of contents, diagrams, and sidebars.

Snap Shot Series: *Mark Twain, Alexander Graham Bell, Albert Einstein, Harry Houdini, Wright Brothers, Marie Curie, Helen Keller, Eleanor Roosevelt, George Washington Carver,* and *Lucy Maud Montgomery*, by Elizabeth MacLead. 2008. Kids Can Press, NY. This biographical series contains text features: table of contents, index, timelines, photographs, captions, and sidebars.

Submarines and Submersibles, by Deborah Lock. 2007. DK Publishing, NY. A simple index, insets, a glossary, and photos teach about the day of a person who works with submarines and other underwater machines and equipment.

Surprise Puppy, by Judith Walker-Hodge. 1998. DK Publishing, NY. This day in the life of a puppy uses labels, insets, and photographs to tell about the parts of his life.

Truck Trouble, by Angela Royston. 1998. DK Publishing, NY. Photographs, labels, and insets help the reader learn about a typical day for a truck driver. Many vehicles are covered.

STRUCTURE: PROCEDURAL

100 Science Experiments, by George Andrews and Kelly Knighton. 2007. Usborne Books, UK. This detailed how-to book contains web links to gain more information on each experiment. It also contains the text features sidebars, pictures with captions, index, glossary, and table of contents.

101 Great Science Experiments: Step-by-Step Guide, by Neil Ardley. 1993. DK Publishing, NY. This is a detailed how-to book that contains the text features sidebars, pictures and captions, a table of contents, and an index.

1-2-3 Draw Cartoon Animals, by Steve Barr. 2002. Peel Productions, Northern Lights Books, OH. Clearly illustrated step-by-step of how to draw the animals.

1-2-3 Draw Pets and Farm Animals, by Fred Levin. 2001. Peel Productions, Northern Lights Books, OH. Clearly illustrated step-by-step of how to draw the animals.

All about Seeds, by Melvin Berger. 1992. Scholastic, NY. This is also a description in that it tells about seeds. It contains how-to projects and do-it-yourself tasks throughout the book. Text access feature include step-by-step directions, picture charts, and labels.

Children's Cookbook, by Katherine Ibbs. 2004. DK Publishing, NY. Step-by-step photographs, insets, headings, a table of contents, and a glossary are used for teaching tasks in this book.

Children's Quick and Easy Cookbook, by Angela Wilkes. 2003. DK Publishing, NY. Photographed table of contents, ingredient list, and steps help this book be reader-friendly.

First Baking Activity Book, by Helen Drew. 2007. DK Publishing, NY. Photographed table of contents, ingredient list, and steps helps this book be reader-friendly.

First Garden Activity Book, by Angela Wilkes. 2008. DK Publishing, NY. This book is a detailed how-to book on how to plant different kinds of seeds and bulbs. Text access features include step-by-step directions, pictures, captions, and photographs.

From Peanuts to Peanut Butter, by Melvin Berger. 1992. Newbridge Communications, US. This book shows the process of how a peanut is turned into peanut butter in the format of a big book. This process is shown through the use of vivid photographs and simple sentences. Text access features include photographs.

From Seed to Plant, by Gail Gibbons. 1991. Holiday House, NY. This book explains in a time order format how a seed becomes a plant. A how-to project on growing a seed is included.

From Tree to Table, by Jill Braithwaite. 2004. Lerner Publications, MN. This book shows the process of how a table is made. This process is explained through vivid photographs and simple paragraphs. Text access feature include photographs, bold print, table of contents, glossary, and index.

Oceans and Seas, by Nicola Davies. See "Structure: Descriptive."

Super Science Concoctions, by Jill Frankel Hauser. 2007. Williamson Books, TN. This is a detailed how-to book with additional facts with each recipe. All experiments explore different areas of science.

The Usborne Big Book of Experiments, by Fiona Johnson. 2007. Usborne Books, UK. This how-to book contains the text access features glossary, index, fun facts, sidebars, pictures with captions, photographs, and diagrams.

The Usborne First Cookbook, by Angela Wilkes. 2006. Usborne, UK. Clear photographed directions, sidebars, headings, and captions.

STRUCTURE: EXPLANATORY

Don't Know Much Series: *The Pilgrims,* by Kenneth C. Davis. 2003. HarperCollins, NY. Other titles in series include *50 States, History, Geography, Civil War.* These explanatory texts contain several text features, such as pictures, captions, diagrams, sidebars, words with definitions, insets, headings, subheadings, and maps.

If You Series: *Colonial Times,* by Ann McGovern. 1997. Scholastic, NY. Other titles include *Civil War* and *American Revolution,* by Kay Moore, and *When Woman Won Their Rights,* by Ann Kamma. This series of books contains text features: maps, labels, photographs, illustrations, and captions.

I Wonder Why Series: *Stars Twinkle,* by Carole Stott. 2003. Kingfisher, MA. This question/answer book contains the text features table of contents, index, pictures, captions, and diagrams.

Now You Know: Question and Answer Book, by Jack Long. 1994. Wishing Well Books, CT. This book explains answers to children's most-asked questions about animals, how things work, their human body, and nature.

Smithsonian Series: *White House, America Flag, Baseball, Extreme Natures, Extreme Aircraft, Extreme Planets, Extreme Stars, Extreme Rocks and Minerals,* and *Extreme Dinosaurs.* 2008. HarperCollins, NY. This series of books is written in a question/answer format that contains web links and the text features photographs, captions, index, table of contents, fun facts, and glossary.

A Walk in the Jungle, by Dorothea DePrisco. 2006. Silver Dolphin Books, CA. The book is in a large board book presentation. Questions about each area of the jungle rain forest are answered throughout the book. The question/answer format and explanations are presented in a lively way to capture young readers' attention.

What Is a Bellybutton? 1993. Time Life, US. This book explains first questions and answers about the human body.

What Is the Tidal Pool? by Ann Hunter. 2000. Houghton Mifflin, MA. This book explains each form of life in the tidal pool through detailed drawings accompanied by a clear explanation of each.

About the Authors

Darla Taylor Miner has been an educator since 1989. She began her career as a classroom teacher at Long Lots School in Westport, Connecticut. During her tenure as a classroom teacher, she realized her love for teaching children how to read and acquired advanced degrees in reading. She moved into the position of reading specialist, which enabled her to create and implement an early intervention program, as well as work with curriculum and provide professional development for the district. In 2000, Darla moved to Race Brook School in Orange, Connecticut. As a reading consultant, Darla continues to implement her early intervention program as well as take a leadership position in the development of curriculum, instruction, and professional development for the district. Upon observing the increasing curriculum demands that classroom teachers face, she has made curriculum mapping and instructional integration a focus—not only to increase student achievement but also to help teachers manage curriculum and make teaching creative. Darla worked with Larry Ainsworth as part of the Connecticut Rigorous Curriculum ELA Design Team to write units of study using the Common Core Standards. Darla received both her undergraduate and advanced degrees at Southern Connecticut State University. She has presented workshops at the state and national levels, including the National Staff Developers Council conferences in Nashville, Tennessee; Dallas, Texas; and St. Louis, Missouri.

Jill Zitnay has been an educator since 1990. She began her career in Fairfield, Connecticut, as a special education teacher. Jill's experience included working with students and teachers from early elementary school through high school. In 2004, Jill became a reading consultant for the Orange Public School system in Connecticut. In her current role, she provides professional development, runs daily data team meetings, and models best practice techniques for teachers in grades K–6. Jill also provides instruction to students and supervises a schoolwide tiered intervention model. Jill's special interest lies in using research and data to develop curriculum, inform teachers, and improve student performance. Jill has written curricula that correspond with the new Common Core Standards in the areas of reading/language arts and writing. Jill received her undergraduate and advanced degrees from Southern Connecticut State University. She has presented workshops at the state and national levels, including the National Staff Development Council conferences in Nashville, Tennessee; Dallas, Texas; and St. Louis, Missouri.